Native Religion under Roman Domination

Deities, springs and mountains in
the north-west of the Iberian Peninsula

Elizabeth A. Richert

BAR International Series 1382
2005

Published in 2016 by
BAR Publishing, Oxford

BAR International Series 1382

Native Religion under Roman Domination

ISBN 978 1 84171 822 4

© E A Richert and the Publisher 2005

The author's moral rights under the 1988 UK Copyright,
Designs and Patents Act are hereby expressly asserted.

All rights reserved. No part of this work may be copied, reproduced, stored,
sold, distributed, scanned, saved in any form of digital format or transmitted
in any form digitally, without the written permission of the Publisher.

BAR Publishing is the trading name of British Archaeological Reports (Oxford) Ltd.
British Archaeological Reports was first incorporated in 1974 to publish the BAR
Series, International and British. In 1992 Hadrian Books Ltd became part of the BAR
group. This volume was originally published by Archaeopress in conjunction with
British Archaeological Reports (Oxford) Ltd / Hadrian Books Ltd, the Series principal
publisher, in 2005. This present volume is published by BAR Publishing, 2016.

Printed in England

BAR titles are available from:

           BAR Publishing
           122 Banbury Rd, Oxford, OX2 7BP, UK
EMAIL   info@barpublishing.com
PHONE +44 (0)1865 310431
FAX   +44 (0)1865 316916
           www.barpublishing.com

Table of Contents

Acknowledgments 1
Introduction 2
Mountain Divinities 3
   Roman Equivalents? *5*
   External Parallels *6*
Aquatic Divinities 6
   Roman Equivalents? *8*
   External Parallels *8*
Protector Divinities 9
   Roman Equivalents? *10*
   External Parallels *11*
Warrior Divinities 11
   Roman Equivalents? *12*
   External Parallels *13*
Other Divinities 13
   Roman Equivalents? *14*
   External Parallels *14*
Sanctuary Sites 15
Conclusion 16
Catalogue I 18
Inscriptions to Indigenous Deites 18
   Conventus Bracaraugustanus *18*
   Uncertain Readings from the Conventus Bracaraugustanus *22*
   Conventus Lucensis *23*
   Uncertain Reading from the Conventus Lucense *26*
   Conventus Asturum *26*
   Uncertain Reading from the Conventus Asturum *28*
Catalogue II 29
Classical Deities in the North-West of Hispania 29
   Conventus Bracaraugustanus *29*
   Uncertain Reading from the Conventus Bracaraugustanus *36*
   Conventus Lucensis *36*
   Unsure Readings from the Conventus Lucense *40*
   Conventus Asturum *40*
   Uncertain Readings from the Conventus Asturum *45*
   Location Unsure in the North-West *45*
Catalogue III 46
Classical Deities with Indigenous Epithets 46
   Conventus Bracaraugustanus *46*
   Uncertain Readings from the Conventus Bracaraugustanus *47*
   Conventus Lucensis *47*
   Uncertain Reading from the Conventus Lucense *47*
   Conventus Austurum *48*
   Location Unsure in the North-West *48*
Appendix I 49
   1. Indigenous Insriptions from Catalogue I *49*
   2. Roman Inscriptions from Catalogue II *50*
   3. Roman Inscriptions with Indigenous Epithets from Catalogue III *51*
   4. Reve Inscriptions from Catalogue I *52*
   5. Jupiter Inscriptions from Catalogues I, II, and III *53*
   6. Nabia Inscriptions from Catalogue I *54*
   7. Nymph Inscriptions from Catalogue II and III *55*
   8. Bandua Inscriptions from Catalogue I *56*
   9. Lar, Lares and Lares Viales Inscriptions from Catalogues II and III *57*
   10. Cosus Inscriptions from Catalogue I *58*
   11. Mars Inscriptions from Catalogues II and III *59*
References 60

Acknowledgments

This analysis on the north-west of the Iberian Peninsula was the basis for my MSc dissertation at the University of Edinburgh. I would like to thank my supervisor from Edinburgh, Dr. Eberhard Sauer, for the guidance and wisdom he shared with me.

During my education in Canada I had the pleasure of studying under Dr. Chris Foley and Dr. Allison Maingon who, along with Cathy Gunderson, I have to credit for awakening within me a passion for antiquity.

I would also like to thank my husband Luc, my parents, Tina and Vincent, and Faye, Chad and Kya for their ongoing love and support, and Jean for her enduring friendship.

Many thanks to all.

Elizabeth Richert

Introduction

Many articles on religion in the north-west of Roman Spain begin by stating Strabo's bold assertion that the indigenous peoples of this region were atheists (3.4.16). Perhaps this quotation derives its popularity from the fact that it is one of the only direct literary references to indigenous worship, or lack there-of, in this corner of the Iberian Peninsula. Or, perhaps its curiosity lies in its completely erroneous nature. It seems likely that the assertion was influenced by the lack of anthropomorphized divinities and monumental cult places manifest in the region. This then was extrapolated into an allegation that the natives worshipped no gods. In fact, this stands in direct opposition to the numerous epigraphic testaments of native divinities that have been preserved in the region (see Cat.I & III). These tell a story of a wide-ranging though ill-defined, nature based indigenous religion that persisted tenaciously throughout the domination of the Romans.

It is this persistence of native religious worship in the north-west of Hispania that will form the focus of this essay. The region in question, the last section of the Iberian Peninsula to be brought under the control of Roman, was first grouped into the province of Lusitania in the late first century BC, though Augustus soon reassigned it to that of Citerior (Tarraconensis) (Keay 1988:46; Curchin 1991:53). It included the three Roman judicial districts of the *Conventus Bracaraugustanus* in the south-west, the *Conventus Lucense* above this in the north-west and the *Conventus Asturum* to the east (Nicols 1987:130). In Diocletian's late third century divisions it became denominated *Gallaecia* (Keay 1988:49,179; Tovar 1989:13). The area, with its prolific scattering of mountains, profound valleys and extensive coastline, would have been an ideal setting for the flourishing of an indigenous religion, intimately linked to the veneration of natural phenomenon. The topography of the region no doubt also led to a degree of isolation which would help account for the fact that this area was not greatly influenced by foreign cultures prior to the Romans (Keay 2001:126). Even Celtic cultural forms, though testified in the region, did not acquire the foothold here that they did in other areas of the Peninsula, such as the Meseta (Caridad Arias 1999:13). Of its topography and isolation Strabo writes bleakly: 'And Northern Iberia, in addition to its ruggedness, not only is extremely cold, but lies next to the ocean, and thus has acquired its characteristic of aversion to intercourse with other countries' he concludes that 'it is an exceedingly wretched place to live in' (3.1.2). Though Strabo is somewhat damning in his comments here, the isolationism and concomitant low degrees of cultural blending prior to the Roman period in this area provides an interesting opportunity to understand the interaction between the new Roman religion and a fairly engrained ancestral, local religion.

In order to assess the degree of survival of this local indigenous religion in our selected region, during the Roman period, this essay will look first and foremost to our most extensive body of available data, the epigraphic record. The Roman practice of dedicating votive altars was a habit which was acquired by the indigenous peoples and, in many cases, adapted to fit their own religion. Though these testaments give us invaluable evidence on the nature of religion in our region of interest it should be kept in mind that they are clearly biased to an elite stratum of the society who openly adopted the cultural forms of their conquerors, namely the Latin language as a linguistic medium and the votive altar as a material medium (Ramirez 1981:226). Unfortunately, those natives who remained unaffected by Roman culture, or could not afford to set up inscriptions, have left behind little record of their religious beliefs. The dating of those inscriptions we do have, moreover, is tenuous and rarely precise (Tranoy 1981:265). Similarly difficult to assess is the actual role or function of the native divinities listed on epigraphic texts. A search for the answer to this question may, though, be aided by inscriptions in which Roman divinities are given native epithets, or through an etymological analysis of the native divinity names themselves (Lambrino 1965:227-8). In the realm of ancient literary sources few mention indigenous religion in Hispania, especially in our area of interest, and even then the validity of their assertions, as in the first mentioned case with Strabo, may be questioned (Blázquez 1983:224). Iconography of native divinities is difficult to come across, as well, due in part to the poor distribution of works in which such pieces are published and in part to the actual lack of such finds in the region (Blázquez 1991:43; Balil 1979:148). A number of noteworthy rock sanctuary sites, nevertheless, have been found in the region which help elucidate indigenous religious practices and which will form a section of this analysis.

To turn back to our prime source of evidence, epigraphy, I have found record of 451 votive inscriptions set up in the north-west of Hispania (see Catologues I, II & III, Maps 1-3). Of these 155 were made out to indigenous divinities, 41 to classical divinities with native epithets, and a further 258 to Roman deities (by which I mean those foreign deities introduced under the Romans, be they Roman, Greek or Oriental in origin). Three of these dedications invoke divinities from more than one category at once and so account for the fact that the numbers of dedications per category are slightly greater in sum than the total number of inscriptions (No.49, Cat.I; No.182, Cat.II; No.37 Cat.III). The majority of native divinities venerated are only named on one occurrence and are, thus, difficult to interpret (Map 1). Some indigenous divinities do nevertheless appear to have held a wider sphere of influence. Cosus was invoked on 15 occasions, Lariberus Breus on 12 (all from Donón, Pontevedra), Bandua on 11 and one possible, Navia/Nabia on 10 and one possible, and Reve on five occasions. It should be noted that the spelling of these divinity names often varies depending on inscription. These indigenous divinities who were worshipped more prolifically suggest that the ancestral religion of the area was not simply a personalized phenomenon but had some common threads that traversed the region.

On the Roman side clustering of dedications is more noticeable. This is especially the case in the *Conventus Asturum* where the strong army presence would have effected this distribution. This *Conventus* thus exhibits a divide between urban centers in which Roman inscriptions cluster and rural areas which are scattered with native epigraphic testaments (compare Maps 1 and 2) (Tranoy 1981:324). In contrast to this, the *Conventus Bracaraugustanus* and the *Conventus Lucense,* to a lesser extent, display a fairly widespread scattering of Roman votive inscriptions throughout the region, both in rural and urban areas (Map 2). Taking the region of the north-west as a whole we can note a number of Roman divinities who appear to have received especially prolific adoration. These include first and foremost Jupiter (and Jupiter Optimus Maximus) with an impressive 117 dedications, followed by the Nymphs with 25 and one possible, the Lares Viales with 23 and 2 possible, the Lar/Lares wth 18 and 1 possible, the Genius with 14, and Mars with 12 and 1 possible dedications. These numbers include both invocations of the divinities on their own and with native epithets. After these in frequency were dedications to Fortuna, Mercury, Diana and Tutela. Though these numbers of Roman divinities are high in comparison to native, it will be shown that many of these classical deities have the distinct flavour of ancestral indigenous gods and quite plausibly represent translations of such deities. It should further be born in mind that the Roman divinities who were most prolifically testified in the north-west of Hispania were also those deities that we find with native epithets (see Catalogue III).

The mixing of indigenous and Roman religious beliefs that will form the focus of this essay has often been referred to as part of the process of 'Romanization' of the conquered peoples. In our post-imperial culture, though, the idea that Romanization was in fact an occurrence in which all things Roman were enforced onto the unsuspecting indigenous population has largely been brought into question. Some scholars have more recently asserted that the natives played a vital role in their own acculturation process (Millett 1990:38). In this view the elite stratum actively adopted aspects of the conquerors culture thereby assisting in the blending of the two cultures. Keay sees this as a 'symbiotic but unequal process,' thus, neither excluding imperial agency or elite adoptions as fueling the process (2001:123). Though James agrees with an active role of the local elite in their own 'Romanization,' he worries that such a view 'over-privileges' the role of this upper stratum of society at the expense of all others (James 2001:205). Jane Webster, for her part, suggests that the indigenous populations were resistant to the adoption of their conquerors' gods and that the native divinities 'were converted to it [the Roman pantheon] by force' (1995:160). For my part, I am inclined to disagree with Webster and follow the viewpoint of Simon Keay, thus taking the perspective that the natives of north-west Hispania underwent a more active form of adaptation to Roman culture, largely fueled by internal adoptions though also affected by imperial initiative. These varying viewpoints will be brought up once again in the conclusion of this essay at which time it will be possible to ascertain what light the material evidence has to shed on this debate.

This analysis will take a bottom-up approach, looking from an indigenous perspective and assessing this group's response to Roman religion. The essay will be laid out thematically focusing on key areas of indigenous cultic veneration in the region including mountain and aquatic cult, and worship of protector and warrior divinities. I do not in any way purport that these categories are comprehensive, but only form a starting point for an analysis of the native religion. An additional section on divinities which do not fit into these aforementioned categories will be added for the sake of completeness. Each section, once having assessed the evidence from the native sphere, will look to see if any Roman equivalents fit into the indigenous pattern of worship. Following this, parallel examples of indigenous religious veneration from elsewhere in the western Empire will be elucidated per section. A final section will be devoted to cult places, especially rock sanctuary sites, and the sacrificial rites that went on at them. In sum, the essay will look to discover the nature of native religion in the north-west of the Iberian Peninsula during the Roman period and its level of endurance. The amount to which Roman religion was selectively adopted by the native elite to fit into their pre-existing model of ancestral worship will also be analyzed.

Mountain Divinities

One of the most pervasive tendencies in north-western Iberian indigenous religion, to judge by the epigraphic record, was the veneration of high places (Albertos Firmat 1974:148). This cult comes as no surprise in an area typified by numerous mountain ranges. These ranges had long been the places-of-choice for native communities. That is, indigenous people had long lived in 'castros,' or fortified hill-top villages, situated on such high spots, many existing fully into Roman times (Vázquez Varela & Acuňa Castroviejo 1992:81). Knowing then that mountains played an integral role in the lives of the native inhabitants in this corner of the Peninsula, how can this be extrapolated to show these people in fact venerated such high places?

We have only a single ancient literary reference which clearly relates to north-western Iberian mountain worship (Lourenço Fontes & Rodríguez Colmenero 1980:21). Justine speaks of a sacred mountain in this region that could not be mined with iron instruments as this was sacrilege (XLIV, III, 6). The exact placement of this mountain in the north-west is difficult to conclude upon though it may well be one of the numerous hills which are today denoted *Monte Sagro* (Sacred Mountain) or *Pico Sagro* (Sacred Peak) (Rodríguez Colmenero 1977:297). This propensity in itself, to name mountains 'sacred,' could possibly have roots in ancient patterns of worship also.

Turning away from the ancient literature, the epigraphic record includes many deity names which either themselves reflect mountain names, or hold epithets that link them to certain peaks. These indigenous mountain divinities became linked to classical deities, Jupiter Optimus Maximus most specifically, which allowed widespread native worship of mountains to persist in the guise of a Roman cult. It is to these epigraphic testaments that I will now turn my attention in order to help elucidate this occurrence.

The fairly well-known native deity Reve, to whom five altars were erected in the *Conventus Bracaraugustanus*, appears to have been a divinity related to mountain worship (Map 4) (Nos.55-59, Cat.I). His name derives from the Germanic root *reu-, reua: rū*, or latin *ruo,* which according to Rodríguez Colmenero signifies: to conduct, run with a rush (impetus), open briskly, etc. (1977:304). The same author suggests this 'violent rush' may relate to thunder, common to mountainous areas (1977:305). Alternatively, Villar sees this deity name as affirming an association between Reve and river veneration (1994-5:247). These two viewpoints need not be at odds with one another as Reve may very well have had multiple aspects, being at once a divinity associated with rivers and mountains (Olivares Pedreño 2000a:198). It is, after all, from the great mountains of north-western Hispania that the numerous rivers stream forth.

One of the altars to Reve, found in Guiâes (Vila Real), links the divinity with the epithet 'Marandicuus' which is evidently a reference to the nearby Sierra de Marâo (No.58, Cat.I) (Olivares Pedreño 2000a:192). Another altar to 'Reve Laraucus' found in Baltar (Ginzo de Limia, Orense, northern Portugal) clearly alludes to the nearby Monte Larouco which rises to some 1538 m (No.57, Cat.I) (Olivares Pedreño 2000a:192). The remaining three altars, though not linked specifically to a mountain in name, all hale from loosely the same mountainous area of *Conventus Bracaraugustanus* as this aforementioned altar to Reve Laraucus. One of these, which venerates 'Reve' on his own, was found also in the region of Ginzo de Limia, near the Serra de Gerês, of which the Monte Larouco forms a part (No.55, Cat.I). Another to 'Reve Ana Baraeco' was located not far west of here, between the Serra de Gerês and the Serra de Peneda, in the area of Bande (No.56, Cat.I). The third was found some thirty kilometres east of Baltar (No.59, Cat.I). All five aforementioned invocations of the indigenous deity Reve, then, relate to mountainous areas, some going so far as to name for us the mountain to which they are linked. Their tendency to cluster in the region around Ginzo de Limia suggests Reve was the sovereign deity of this mountainous zone.

This, though, does not appear to have been Reve's sole area of influence. Outside our region of study, in Lusitania, more evidence of a cult to Reve can be found. At the rock sanctuary site of Cabeço das Fraguas (Pousafoules do Bispo, Sabugal) Reve was named along with four other native deities (Rodríguez Colmenero 1993:105). This inscription, which is written in the native Lusitanian language, explains which animals were to be sacrificed to each deity (Alarcâo 1988, Vol.I:97). Like all the previously mentioned invocations of Reve, this rock inscription also was located near to a mountain range, the Sierra de Estrella (Rodríguez Colmenero 1993:105). Clearly then, Reve appears to be a native divinity of widespread adoration who was related to great mountain peaks. As such he appears as a native equivalent of Jupiter, possibly also imbued with the concomitant celestial aspects of this great Roman god.

Mountain cult in our region did not end with the worship of Reve though. Other native and classical divinities also play a role in this cult. For example, the Larouco Mountain which was venerated in combination with Reve also appears in epigraphy on its own. Near the mountain an inscription was found to 'Larauco Deo Maximo' (No.36, Cat.I) along with various other illegible altars and a dedication to Jupiter Optimus Maximus (No.37, Cat.II) (Tranoy 1981:281). The dedication to Laraucus attributes this mountain divinity with an epithet characteristic of Jupiter (Lourenço Fontes 1980:7). This, taken along with the proximity of this altar to that of Jupiter Optimus Maximus, seems to suggest that Jupiter came to be associated with the divinity of this mountain.

The nearby native rock sanctuary site of Pena Escrita (Vilar de Perdizes, Montalegre) may well also have been a manifestation of this cult. This sacrificial site was decorated with what appear, according to Rodríguez Colmenero, to be crescent moons or horseshoes oriented in various directions; a pre-Roman style of adornment found in abundance in the north-west (1993:75-6). On the south face of the rock, Rodríguez Colmenero interprets an inscription as: 'le(gionis) VII G(eminae) P(iae) (followed by an inverted C)' (1993:76). This testifies to the use of the rock sanctuary during the Roman period when presumably the natives, including those who had joined the Roman army, persisted in their ancestral traditions of worship and sacrifice. Due to this rock sanctuary's proximity to the inscriptions to Laraucus and Jupiter Optimus Maximus (No.36, Cat.I & No.37,Cat.II), and its location facing the Monte Larauco, it seems quite plausible that this sanctuary was where the indigenous people of the region made their offerings and sacrifices to the great divinity of this mountain.

Yet a further inscription to 'Larouco' attests to the powerful sacred nature of this mountain. This dedication from Curral de Vacas south-east of the mountain, near the

Roman city of Aquae Flaviae, was dedicated by the indigenous woman, Ama, daughter of Pitilus, for her husband (No.37, Cat.I) (Rodríguez Colemenero & Lourenço Fontes 1980:26). Overall then, this mountain clearly had a strong sacred importance. It continued to be venerated in Roman times, in all directions, either on its own, or double-named with native Reve, or Roman Jupiter.

Mountain cult does not appear to have been peculiar to the *Conventus Bracaraugustanus* but is also evidenced in the more easterly *Conventus Asturum*. Here, a dedication to 'Jupiter Ladico' inscribed on a rock found in Codos de Laroco (Orense), between Puebla de Trives and Barco de Valdeorras, was once thought to be an invocation of the great Larouco Mountain (Albertos Firmat 1974:149). With the discovery of the earlier mentioned altars to 'Larocus,' though, it seems unlikely that the 'Ladicus' altar was also a derivation of the mountain name. Albertos Firmat suggests instead that this altar may relate to the peak of the Cabeza de Manzaneda, which reaches some 1778 m, and to which the altar is more closely situated (1974:149). A second altar from the same locale has been interpreted by some as another veneration of Jupiter Ladicus. These were both set up by an Imperial freedman (Nos.32 & 33, Cat.III). Though they cannot be assuredly attached to the veneration of a specific mountain, their location and association with Jupiter make it possible for us to assume they may well relate to this cult.

In the mountainous zone of the north of the province of León, also in the *Conventus Asturum*, a further altar linked to mountain worship was found. Here, in the region of the hills of Pajares and of Piedrafita, near the community of Candanedo de Fenar, a dedication was made to Jupiter Candamius (No.31, Cat.III) (Albertos Firmat 1974:152). Not only was this altar situated in a high location, it also refers directly to the Monte Candamio (Olivares Pedreño 2000a:191). To judge by place names in the region that appear to derive from this deity name, such as Candemora (Reinosa, Santander) and Candiano (Laredo, Santander), it seems that the divinity of the Monte Candamio was well known throughout the region (Blázquez 1991:58). A further dedication to 'Jupiter Optimus Maximus Candiedus' of imprecise provenance in the north-west also seems to reflect the root of this mountain name (No.40, Cat.III). The indigenous epithets of both dedications, according to Albertos Firmat, relate to the root *kand-* meaning to shine, burn, or gleam, which she suggests refers to a mountain which shines due to its height and snow-capped peaks that reflect the sun (1974:152).

One final dedication from this *Conventus* which invoked 'Jupiter Optimus Maximus Anderon,' is worth mention (No.39, Cat.III). Though this deity name does not appear to link specifically to any modern mountain name the epithet Anderon, possibly deriving from the Vasco-Iberian *andi-* = great, large ('grande'), may in itself suggest an association between this divinity and great heights (Caridad Arias 1999:153).

Of the evidence for mountain cult mentioned thus far we have seen mountains venerated by their name alone, double-named with indigenous Reve or Roman Jupiter, or simply venerated under either of these two deity names without an attached epithet making special reference to the peak in question. To this evidence must be added a link between Roman Mars and mountain worship. In the *Conventus Asturum*, in the region of La Bañeza, rises the impressive Monte Tileno. This great height was venerated as Mars Tilenus on a silver plaque found at the villa of *Los Villares*, in Quintana del Marco, nearby the mountain (No.34, Cat.III) (Albertos Firmat 1974:150). On the opposite side of the mountain a dedication which venerated it on its own as 'Tillenus' was found at S. Martinho de Viloria (No.150, Cat.I) (Tranoy 1981:306; Albertos Firmat 1974:151). Jupiter it seems, then, was not the only Roman deity to be absorbed into indigenous mountain worship in north-west Iberia.

Roman Equivalents?
We have already seen a great deal of evidence showing that Roman deities became incorporated into indigenous north-western Iberian mountain cult. Jupiter especially, being himself a divinity of mountains with strong celestial attributes, came to easily be associated with this native cult (Albertos Firmat 1974:148). The association of Jupiter with mountain names does not suggest a native adoption of this deity in his aspect as the great god of the Roman state, Capitoline Jupiter. It instead reflects his acceptance as a divinity related to this aspect of nature. In the numerous dedications to Jupiter Optimus Maximus found in this corner of the Peninsula, then, we must assume that at least a proportion of these –those not dedicated in military or highly urbanized contexts –may reflect indigenous mountain worship.

There were 117 dedications made to Jupiter and Jupiter Optimus Maximus in our region of interest. 20 of these made reference to the good health of the Emperor, had Latin epithets such as Capitolinus, or included various other classical deities in their dedication. These then relate to purely Roman cult, often Imperial cult, and cannot be thought to reflect indigenous worship. Putting these 20 aside then, the remaining 97 dedications were made primarily in the *Conventus Bracaraugustanus* (63 dedications, or 64.9%), followed by the *Conventus Asturum* (18 dedications, or 18.6%) and then the *Conventus Lucensis* (13 dedications, or 13.4%). Three further inscriptions were of unsure provenance in the north-west (see Map 5).

These 97 dedications made out to Jupiter or Jupiter Optimus Maximus were not found primarily in the *Conventus* capitals, but appear to have been a more rural phenomenon. Only 9 of the 94 Jupiter inscriptions with known provenances (or 9.6% of all inscriptions) were located in, or in the immediate vicinity of, these capitals;

two in the *Conventus Lucense*, three in *Asturum* and four in *Bracaraugustanus*. This distribution of Jupiter inscriptions again suggests they were an indigenous phenomenon, and unlikely to have been associated with the Roman state god and Imperial cult. It appears, also, that only 9 of the 97 were set up by dedicators with *tria-nomina* (a hallmark of either a Roman or a native well integrated into Roman culture). Instead 54 (or 55.7%) of the inscriptions were made by dedicators without *tria-nomina*, and in the remaining 34 (or 35.1%) of the inscriptions the dedicators name either was never inscribed or could no longer be made out. This fact again elucidates the non-official nature of these inscriptions and suggests to me that they may well be testaments of indigenous worship which was realized through the Roman epigraphic tradition, and through the translation of a native divinity --perhaps a mountain deity-- into its Roman equivalent.

Not all these 97 invocations of Jupiter or Jupiter Optimus Maximus made in this corner of the Peninsula can be thought to relate to mountain cult, and it is difficult and tenuous for us to assume what native deity, if any, an indigenous venerator was in his/her mind worshipping when he/she set up an invocation to Jupiter. A few points, though, may be made with more certainty. It can be told from indigenous inscriptions alone that mountains were venerated. We know that Jupiter is a sky-god and have also seen that he was often double-named with indigenous mountain divinities. It thus seems a plausible conclusion that Jupiter, without a native epithet, came to be a continuation of this indigenous cult of high places. This does not exclude the possible association of Jupiter with other types of native divinities though.

External Parallels
Elsewhere on the Peninsula, in other mountainous zones, indigenous deities of high places were also attested. We have seen that the indigenous mountain divinity Reve was worshipped at the rock sanctuary of Cabeço das Fraguas. At the 'Montaña Escrita' of Peñalba de Vilastar in Celtiberian central Spain an inscription tells that the great Celtic deity Lugus was worshipped on the summit here (Curchin 2004:172). Sopeña Genzor takes this specific native sanctuary site to be one of the most important examples in which a mountain is consecrated as a place of exchange between human and divine in the Celtic world (1995:229). A dedication to 'Tullonius' from Rioja appears to relate to the nearby Monte Toloño which rises to some 1271 meters (Albertos Firmat 1974:155). Another to 'Dercetius' found in the land of the *Berones*, near the Iberian Cordillera seems to also be associated with local mountain cult (CIL II 5809; Albertos Firmat 1974:153). Sacred mountains, then, appear to have been scattered throughout the Iberian topography of the Roman age.

This phenomenon of mountain veneration was not limited to the Iberian Peninsula but was well attested throughout the Celtic world (Curchin 2004:172). In the Pyrenees, for example, on the Mont Sacon (1541m) a series of altars were found depicting varying imagery including human figures, vegetal growth, and often swastikas and disks. Though most of these altars did not contain inscriptions, one was dedicated to Jupiter Optimus Maximus (Fouet & Souton 1963:283-4,287). The placement of these altars, their indigenous style decoration, and the link to Jupiter all suggest these were manifestations of mountain worship. Likewise, in the whole of Gaul sanctuaries occupying mountain summits have been found dedicated to Jupiter, Mars and Mercury (Thevenot 1968:218). Livy speaks of a peoples who inhabited an area of the Alps in Gaul who considered themselves to have been named by '…that deity whose sanctuary is established on their very summit and whom the mountaineers call Poeninus' (XXI.38.9). Votive plaques from this site, called Grand-St.-Bernard, have been found made out to Jupiter Poeninus and a statuette of Jupiter has also been recovered (Prieur 1976:646). This is only one of many sacred peaks from the region of the Alps whose worship was linked to that of Jupiter and his native Gallic equivalent. Remnants of this worship can still be seen today in such mountain names as *Mont Joux, Montjovet,* and *Montjoie* from this area (Prieur 1976:646).

It will not suit the aims of this essay to explore all occurrences of mountain veneration in the western Empire. Suffice it to say, it was not a phenomenon isolated to north-west Iberia. It appeared in other mountainous regions in Roman Spain and in Gaul, as well as throughout the Celtic world (Curchin 2004:172). In the north-west of Hispania this cult persisted robustly in the Roman period. The towering peaks and the impressive storms and lightening bolts which emanated from them seem to have continued to be looked upon with reverence by the natives. Though Jupiter Optimus Maximus was venerated in official contexts, and quite likely was introduced to the north-west of Iberia through military personnel and other officials, this deity clearly was brought under the umbrella of indigenous nature worship.

Aquatic Divinities

The worship of high places in the north-west of the Iberian Peninsula suggests that nature was an important element of indigenous religion in this region. This concept is further upheld by a series of deities from the area who relate to streams, oceans or most commonly thermal springs. This cult of waters preceded the introduction of Roman aquatic deities here by many centuries (Santos Junior & Cardozo 1953:56). It also seems to have persisted past the Roman period to judge by 6th c. writer Saint Martin of Braga's *De Correctione Rusticorum* in which the author laments the custom of venerating rivers, springs and the Nymphs, in general, in the north-west of Roman Spain (8.10-15). As with mountain cult, the topography of the region undoubtedly also was a key factor in the prominence of the cult of aquatic deities. This corner of the Peninsula is ringed on two sides by the Atlantic Ocean, as well as having a diverse network of rivers streaming down from the mountains that shape its terrain. Some aquatic deities appear to relate in name to a specific river or area while others are more widespread divinities, relating to various different springs or rivers in the region, or in the western Empire. A look at native aquatic deities and the Roman equivalents with which they came to be associated will help us in understanding an important part of the indigenous concept of the world of the divine.

'Nabia,' as the people of the *Conventus Bracaraugustanus* knew her, or 'Navia,' as the people of the *Conventus Lucensis* referred to her, was a widely venerated aquatic deity in the north-west of Hispania (see Map 6). Her name relates to the great Navia River which runs along the east border of the *Conventus Lucensis* (Blázquez 1983:294). Of the 155 indigenous inscriptions from the region 10 and 1 possible, or 7.1% of the inscriptions were made to this divinity. Of the 10, 6 were found in the *Conventus Bracaraugustanus* and 4 and one possible in the *Conventus Lucensis*. This may not seem to be a great number of inscriptions but it is worth keeping in mind that the epigraphic record for this area is made up mostly of deities appearing only once. Only four other native divinities (Bandua, Reve, Cosus, Lariberus Breus) have a comparable number of inscriptions dedicated to them in the region.

One of the most interesting locations in which Nabia was worshipped was the Fonte do Idolo, located near the ancient *Conventus* capital, Bracara Augusta. Here in a small open area, reached off the Rua do Raio, was found a medium sized rock outcrop with a spring flowing from its base. On the escarpment of the rock reliefs and inscriptions could be made out (Rodríguez Colmenero 1993:81). An inscription tells us that the man who had the shrine built was from the village of Arcobriga, the *gens* of Ambimogidi and called Celius (Alarcão 1988, Vol.I:96). A votive altar to the goddess Nabia was set up here by a woman called Rufina (No. 47, Cat.I). Another inscription invoked the hitherto unknown deity 'Tongonabiagus' in whose name the deity name 'Nabia' is clearly embedded (No.63, Cat.I) (Tranoy 1980:76). Tranoy proposes that this deity name is an invention of the dedicator, who he believes is from Lusitania, combining a local tutelary deity of the dedicators place of origin with an indigenous deity common to the area of Bracara Augusta (1980:77). Rodríguez Colmenero is more inclined to see 'Tongonabiagus' as the name of a *gentilitate* who themselves sought protection in the deity Nabia (1993:88-9). Be this as it may, there clearly is some reference being made to the native spring deity Nabia in this inscription. Also found at the site was a rock sculpture depicting a togate figure (god or donor?) and another of a male bust. The male bust has been interpreted as a depiction of the dedicator Celius Fronto. The togate figure has invoked varying hypotheses from Blázquez who takes it to be an indigenous river deity depicted in classical guise to Rodríguez Colmenero who thinks it more likely to be a goddess of plenty, such as Fortuna (Blázquez 2001:195; Rodríguez Colmenero 1993:88). Suffice it to say that the depiction, again, likely has some relevance to Nabia, the deity venerated at the site, but is not in a sufficient condition to be elucidated any further. This site, then, clearly links the deity Nabia to indigenous spring worship.

An additional noteworthy inscription to Nabia comes from Marecos, near Penafiel (No. 49, Cat.I). It tells us what should be sacrificed to Nabia, Jupiter, (…)urgo and Lida, as well as the place of the sacrifice, the date and the organizers (Tranoy 1981:282; Olivares Pedreño 2000b:67-8). In it Nabia is given the epithet 'Corona' and invoked as protector nymph of the Danigi (Alarcão 1988, Vol.I & II: 93,1/457). This dedication was found in the south-west corner of the *Conventus Bracaraugustanus* where another three altars to her were also located (Nos. 45,46,47, Cat.I). The area seems, then, to have been especially fond of this native aquatic deity. Though it cannot be definitively proven that each of the ten dedications to Nabia/Navia were in fact venerating her as an aquatic deity, the association of her with a nymph on the Marecos inscription along with her obvious link to the sacred spring of the Fonte do Idolo, and the relation of her name to the Navia river suggests that her worship was related to the cult of sacred waters.

Two other native deities who are attributed with aquatic characteristics, and for whom there is evidence in north-western Hispania, are Bormanicus and Coventina. The deity name Bormanicus relates to the Indo-European root *bher(v)* = to boil, agitate, and to the Indo-Germanic *gvher* = hot. It also is similar to the Latin *ferveo* and Greek Θερός (Diez de Velasco 1985:72). This deity was venerated on two inscriptions from Caldas de Vizuela (Nos. 15 & 16, Cat.I) (Olivares Pedreño 2000b:68). The 'Caldas' of this place-name may relate to the Latin term *Calidae* or *Aquae Calidae,* quite possibly referring to the existence of thermal waters at the site in Roman times (Diez de Velasco 1985:70). This notion is strengthened by the existence of such waters at the town today as well as by the recovery of Roman bath installations from the site (Diez de Velasco 1985:87). Caldas de Vizuela is located in the region of the south-west of the *Conventus Bracaraugustanus,* as with the aforementioned four altars to Nabia, further emphasizing the importance of water cult, or the cult of therapeutic waters, in this zone. From the *Conventus Lucensis* we find two dedications to Coventina; inscribed as 'Cohventina' and 'Cuhve(tena) Berralogecus' (Nos. 81 & 82, Cat.I). Both Coventina and Bormanicus (as Bormanus) are attested elsewhere in the western Empire in relation to thermal springs. This point will be further explored in the section on external parallels.

In Caldas de Reyes, in an area in which the foundations of an ancient thermal spring exist, an inscription shows that the locals worshipped a deity called 'Edovius' (No.90, Cat.I) (Albertos Firmat 1974:147; López

Cuevillas 1988:294). This deity name, according to González Pardo, signifies 'he who heats the water' (1965:53). Another deity varyingly interpreted as 'Suldis ...Antugaicis,' 'Sulen Santu Gaicis' and 'Suleae Nantugicae' is thought by Tranoy to have been a protector of the springs in the region of Condado (Padrenda, Orense) (No.61, Cat.I) (Tranoy 1981:277; Rodríguez Colmenero 1977:309; IRG IV 98). This goddess name is similar to 'Sulis,' an indigenous healing/spring deity worshipped, along with Minerva, at a sanctuary in Bath (Britain).

Springs were not the only waters that were divinized in the north-west of Hispania though. For example, at the confluence of the Duoro and Támega Rivers an indigenous man named Cumelus vowed, and his son erected, an altar to the deity of the Támega River, called 'Tameobrigus' (No.62, Cat.I) (Tranoy 1981:277). Another dedication to 'Durius' alludes to the divinity of the Duoro River (No.34, Cat.I). The inscription was located in Porto which is situated where this great river spills out into the North Atlantic Ocean (López Cuevillas 1988:294). The indigenous peoples of north-west Hispania, thus, avidly worshipped the life giving forces of water. This worship was not only realized through native deities but also became linked to Roman equivalents.

This process of relating indigenous aquatic cult to foreign deities can be seen in an early state of development in two inscriptions to the Nymphs in which these deities are given native epithets (Nos. 22 & 23, Cat.III). The epithets of both appear to relate in name to waters. In the first dedication to the 'Nymphae Lupianae,' the root *Lup-* is thought by Blázquez to refer to water. The epithet 'Silonis' of the second appears to relate to the river Sil which finishes in the Miño some kilometres north of the appearance of this altar, and into which river votive arms were offered (Blázquez 1975:120 & 1991:64; Rodríguez Colmenero 1977:303). These two altars, both erected by females, show an adoption of the Nymphs as they fit well into the persistent traditional indigenous water cult. The Nymphs then came to hold an important position in the pantheon of the region on their own.

Roman Equivalents?

The Nymphs were female divinities of the classical world who inhabited forests, mountains and especially springs, and who symbolized creative forces, fertility and the renovation of life (Santos Junior & Cardozo 1953:54; Rodríguez Colmenero 1977:300). These aquatic deities were found near thermal waters in the mountainous zones of the Pyrenees extending to Navarra, Galicia, northern Portugal, Castilla y León and Extremadura (Mayer & Rodà 1986:295-6). A look at the epigraphic record for our region will underscore their prominence here. Including the two aforementioned dedications to the Nymphs with epithets, 25 (and one possible) inscriptions were made out to these aquatic deities ranking them second behind Jupiter as the most prolific Roman divinities in the region (see Map 7). A third of the dedications to the Nymphs, where the dedicators gender is known, were made by females or by a male and a female (in one case). As females are dedicators of only 1/10 of the overall dedications from the region, it is possible that the nymphs held a more important place in the worship of women.

The majority of the dedications to the Nymphs have been found in the *Conventus Bracaraugustanus* (13 inscriptions and one possible), followed by the *Conventus Lucensis* (9 inscriptions) and *Asturum* (3 inscriptions). This pattern fits well with the general distribution of indigenous aquatic dedications. That said, it should be borne in mind that this may also only be a reflection of the overall distribution of inscriptions in which the *Conventus Bracaraugustanus* attested the highest percentage (49.7%), followed by the *Conventus Lucense* (25.5%), *Asturum* (23.5%), and those dedications of unknown provenance in the north-west (1.3%). The Romans not only venerated the cult of waters under the denomination of the Nymphs, but also under various other divinities. A double-named dedication from the *Conventus Asturum* to 'Fontis Aginees(is) Genius,' whose name has been interpreted in a number of ways, relates to a combination of native and classical veneration of water (No.30, Cat.III). The dedication to this deity was found engraved on a rock that towered over a spring which to this day continues to feed the thermal baths of Boñar (Tranoy 1981:305). Fortuna also appears to have been related to aquatic cult at least on two occurrences, from the *Conventus Asturum*. In the first of these she is referred to as 'Fortuna Balneari (of the Baths)' and the second is set up by a bath operator (Nos. 195 & 196, Cat.II). Both of these, though, were set up dedicators with *tria-nomina*, one from a military camp, and thus it seems tenuous and perhaps wholly erroneous to suggest they relate to indigenous worship. The nymphs, on the other hand, do appear to hide a continued native worship of sacred waters. This idea is given credence by the association of the Nymphs with indigenous epithets, as well as the proliferation of Nymph dedications in regions where indigenous water deities were most common. Also the clear persistence in worship of native aquatic deities suggests there was a developed aquatic cult into which the Nymphs could easily be fit.

External Parallels

No other part of the Iberian Peninsula saw the same proliferation of dedications to the Nymphs as the north-west, though these deities were venerated on inscriptions from the west, center and south-east of Hispania (Lambrino 1965:234). Curchin records nine dedications to the Nymphs from central Spain, and Martial mentions a 'mild lake of the Nymphs' near *Bibilis* in Celtiberia (1.49.10; Curchin 2004:172,246). From the area of the thermal waters of Baños de Montemayor (Cáceres) were found three altars to the Nymphae Caparenses (Alvorado Gonzalo, *et al.* 1998:6). Similarly, evidence of indigenous aquatic divinities has been found elsewhere on the Peninsula. For example, the Ibero River was venerated in San Martín de Trevejo (Alvorado Gonzalo *et al.* 1998:6). Near Salamanca at Retorillo the Yeltes River was likewise worshipped as 'Aquae Elete(n)ses' (Albertos Firmat 1974:147). A Lusitanian man called *Boutius* offered a dedication to the north-western aquatic divinity Nabia (CIL II 756). Furthermore, a patera was found in Oñates (Guipúzcoa) dedicated to the spring deity 'Salus Umeritana,' and including a depiction of this anthropomorphic native aquatic deity (Fig 3) (Blázquez 1991:44-5). It appears, then, that the persistence of indigenous water cult was not isolated to the north-west corner of the Iberian Peninsula.

Both Gaul and Britain have produced much evidence of native and Roman aquatic cult, including some interesting parallels with the north-west of Roman Spain. Bormanicus, attested on two altars from Caldas de Vizuela in our region, was honoured in Gaul under the denomination 'Bormanus' and 'Bormana' at sites with thermal waters and is also related to the Gallic spring deity 'Borvo' (Tranoy 1981:269). Coventina was well known to Britain where, in Carrawburgh on Hadrian's Wall, fourteen dedications were made to her. On two of these she is double-named with a Nymph which suggests that she too was an aquatic deity (Birley 1986:45-6). Unfortunately, outside of Carrawburgh the Galician dedications to this deity are the only others known in the Empire, apart from a single inscription from Narbonne, in southern France (AE 1950, no.49). It, thus, remains uncertain whether they definitively relate to the same deity or whether this is just an act of extreme coincidence (Allason-Jones & McKay 1985:3-6). All the same, the worship of Bormanicus/Bormanus and Coventina in the three areas attests to sustained native veneration of aquatic deities over a wide geographical area.

This cult is evidenced further in Britain by the therapeutic spring of Sulis Minerva, at Bath, and the sanctuary of Mars Nodons at Lydney Park, overlooking the Severn River; both Romano-indigenous cultic locations in which healing may have been linked to water (Alcock 1965:5; Wheeler & Wheeler 1932:1). Also, some nine dedications from the region worship the nymphs (Birley 1986:36). These are not the only aquatic deities on the island though. The epithet 'Condatis' given to Mars on three (and one possible) inscriptions from Britain relates to the Gallic for 'watersmeet,' the Latin version of which is 'confluens' (RIB 731,1024,1045; Hassall & Tomlin 1978:475-6; Alcock 1965:4). Alcock takes this to mean Mars Condatis was a god who presided over areas in which two streams converged (1965:4). We therefore may witness evidence of native water cult in Britain, as in Gaul and various locations in Iberia.

Protector Divinities

Another considerable proportion of the divinities attested in the north-west of Hispania fall under the category of tutelary gods, invoked as protectors of peoples or places. Most of these deities are only inscribed on a single inscription and thus are quite difficult, if not impossible in cases, to firmly categorize (Alarcão 1988, Vol.I:94-5). An exception to this is the native deity Bandua. This indigenous deity was recorded on 11, and one possible, inscriptions from north-western Iberia (Map 8) (Nos.6-14,69,79,80, Cat.I). Like those to Nabia, dedications to Bandua tend to cluster in the *Conventus Bracaraugustanus* (9 and one possible in this *Conventus*, 2 in *Lucense*). Unlike the distribution of Nabia altars though, those to Bandua do not appear in the southwest of the *Conventus,* but instead are fairly scattered in all other parts of the region with a notable proportion in the area of Ginzo de Limia.

The deity-name Bandua appears to relate to the Indo-European *bhendh,* meaning 'to tie or bind,' and so emphasizing this divinities protective aspect and ties to the various communities (Blanco Freijeiro 1977:14). The nature of Bandua is further elucidated by a patera from Cáceres, outside our area, which depicts Bandua Araugelensis as Tyche-Fortuna, whose attributes coincide with Tutela (Blázquez 1983:295-6; Rodríguez Colmenero 1977:311). Some of the epithets attached to Bandua such as *Aetobricus, Lansibrica* and *Virubricus* include the suffix *bricus-,* similar to *brigus-,* which is a common Celtic denomination for a community found throughout the region (Fernández Castro 1995:350). This would give weight again to the notion of Bandua as a protector of communities. Likewise, the very fact that on all but 3 of the 11 dedications Bandua was given a native epithet implies that the deity-name was being qualified to relate to the people or place which this divinity was invoked to protect. Thus, Bandua can be seen as a wide-spread protective deity, invoked as the personal guardian of various sites or peoples.

Many other deity names from the north-west allude to the protective character of the divinity invoked. The deity 'Albocelus' is inscribed on an altar from Vilar de Maçada (Vila Real), in the *Conventus Bracaraugustanus* (No.2, Cat.I). This seems to refer to a topographic name which is found in Ptolemy (II.6.49) and the Antonine Itinerary (434.7) (Tranoy 1981:269). A dedication to 'Crougintoudigoe,' from the same *Conventus* unites within the deity-name, the group of people called the *Teuta-* with the term *Crougin-* meaning hill or high-place (No.26, Cat.I) (Tranoy 1981:274). Just as the *–brigus* ending may be taken to relate to a place-name so too does the *–eicus* ending of some inscriptions seem to relate to topographical locales. Following this idea Tranoy takes an inscription to 'Moelius Mordoneicus' and another to 'Torolus Gombiceigus' to be invocations of protective deities relating to communities or places (Nos.41 & 64, Cat.I) (1981:276,278). Yet a further possible tutelary deity is 'Deus Vacodonnaegus.' This native god was venerated collectively and officially by the *Res publica Asturica Augusta,* on an inscription from La Milla del Río (near Astorga) (No.153, Cat.I) (Mangas 1998:126-7). This testifies to a persistent belief in the ancestral protective divinity of the place.

Not only were indigenous deities linked to places, but they were also adored as protectors of specific groups of peoples. In this vein, Rufus, the son of Flavus, set up an inscription to 'Calaica' who is likely to have been a tutelary divinity of the *Callaeci* (No.18, Cat.I) (Tranoy 1981:271). An inscription, similarly, was made to the 'Lares Callaeci,' along with a number of other classical divinities; evidencing a true mixing of traditions (No.182, Cat.II). An inscription to 'Poemana' may relate to the Germanic group called the Poemani, a people who were known to the Iberian Penninsula from around 600BC (No.111, Cat.I) (Vilas, Le Roux & Tranoy 1979:33-4). As such attestations of tutelary deities continue we run the risk of conveniently unloading many unknown divinities into this category along the way (Alarcâo 1988, Vol.I:94). That said, seeing many of the single occurrence divinities as relating to a tribe or community seems logical to some extent as this provides an answer for their appearance in only one locale (at least until more evidence is found that better elucidates their nature).

What appears to have been an important sanctuary of a protective divinity was found at Monte Facho de Donón (Hio, Pontevedra) (Baňos & Pereira-Menaut 1998:21). Here twelve altars were made out to the divinity Lariberus Breus (whose name is inscribed with a number of different spellings) (Nos. 92-103, Cat.I). On a thirteenth altar which was found with these, though the name of the deity venerated is missing, the dedicator is recorded as being 'Aebur[i]na' --a Celtic name common to the Peninsula often occurring as 'Aebura' (Baňos & Pereira 1998:26; CIRG II 13). None of the other altars record the names of their dedicators. The central nucleus of the deity-name, *Breus,* may derive from the Celtic *Brig-,* the Gallic *Bre-* or the Irish *Bri-,* meaning 'hill,' or some other word relating to height and extent. Thus, Baňos and Pereira-Menaut suggest tentatively that *Breus* could translate as *'El Grande'* (or 'the Great One') (1998:29). The 'Lar' portion of the name may relate to the Roman Lares who were themselves protective deities, and thus confirm this deity's function as a protector of this high spot (Baňos & Pereira-Menaut 1998:29). He could likewise, then, be added to our previous list of mountain divinities. In essence, though, many of the aforementioned divinities of specific mountains, springs, rivers, or such natural phenomenon can also be taken as tutelary deities of specific locales. The lines of definition blur somewhat here, but this itself emphasizes the strong tendency of native north-western Iberian religion to hold a link between the divine and its relevance to the land, its topography and peoples.

Roman Equivalents?

Perhaps the most prescient way to come to understand the worship of tutelary deities in our area of interest is to turn to those examples where Roman and native meet. On fourteen altars (and a possible fifteenth) Roman Lar or Lares were given native epithets (Nos. 6-19, 26, Cat.III & No.182, Cat.II). This was a phenomenon limited to the *Conventus Bracaraugustanus,* apart from a single dedication from the *Conventus Lucense* that venerated a number of classical divinities along with the 'Lares Callaeci' (No.182, Cat.II). Also five, and a possible sixth, dedications were made to the classical Genius with indigenous surnames attached (Nos. 1-4, 28, 30, Cat. III). Four of these were found in the *Conventus Bracaraugustanus,* and one in each of the other two *Conventus.* One further Roman protective divinity, Tutela, is attested with native epithets on four altars, two from each of the *Conventus Bracaraugustanus* and *Asturum* (Nos. 24,25,35,36, Cat. III). A notable majority of the double-named dedications to such divinities therefore appear in the *Conventus Bracaraugustanus,* with an almost complete absence of such dedications in the *Conventus Lucense.* For its part the *Conventus Lucense* displays a large number of dedications to the Lares Viales, showing that it was not adverse to the adoption of Roman tutelary deities (Beltrán Lloris 1992:63).

It is through the double-named dedications that we most clearly see evidence for a continued indigenous veneration of deities linked to places and peoples. Many of the epithets attached to Lar or Lares dedications seem to relate to well known surnames from the region (Beltrán Lloris 1992:66-7; Tranoy 1981:303). Untermann mentions that the suffixes –ico and –aeco, may suggest an epithet is an adjective relating a generic deity to a specific clan or family (1965:11-13). Following this logic many of the Lar and Lares inscriptions, such as Lar Cariecus, Lar Circeiebaecus Proeniaecus, Lar Pemaneiecus, Lares Burici, Lares Erredici, Lares Cerenaeci, etc, may relate to families or clans. In the dedication to the 'Lar Sefius' the epithet appears to relate to the people called the *Saefes* who are mentioned in Avienus as having been inhabitants of central Lusitania (Ora Marit. 195 &199; Lambrino 1965:233). Thus the divine, in the north-west of Hispania, was closely linked to the region's inhabitants.

Lambrino has suggested that the association of indigenous surnames with the Lares was an initial step in the adoption of these deities into the north-west of Hispania. They then, according to the French researcher, came to be venerated alone or under the denomination of Lares Viales without losing their ancestral significance (Lambrino 1965:233-4). One flaw appears, though, when assessing this argument. The Lares Viales do not seem to have been ushered in, in the *Conventus Lucensis,* by dedications to the Lares with native epithets serving as liaison for this new cult (see Map 9). In fact, the aforementioned *Conventus* appears to have quite simply adopted the Lares Viales as a new way of representing their native deities, with no intermediary. On the contrary, the *Conventus Bracaraugustanus,* though displaying a large number of dedications to the Lares with native epithets exhibits many fewer dedications to the Lares Viales. Tranoy explains this phenomenon by arguing that the inhabitants of the *Conventus Lucense* were more 'Romanized' than those of the *Conventus*

Bracaraugustanus and thus more apt to make a quick transition to the classical equivalents of their deities without clinging to their old indigenous denominations (1981:323-4). Without concluding either way on this point, Beltrán Lloris wisely notes that what is important here is that both forms of venerating the Lares appear to represent continued local cult (1992:64). Clearly, in their worship of protector divinities both the *Conventus Bracaraugustanus* and *Lucense* followed their own regional trends, both, though, adhering to the nature of the ancestral religion. In the *Conventus Asturum*, in contrast, neither the Lares nor the Lares Viales gained a significant foothold. We must assume that the natives who continued to worship tutelary divinities here decided not to represent these gods under the denomination of their Roman equivalents.

Be this as it may, it is clear that the Lares and Lares Viales were worshipped prolifically in the north-west of Hispania. This fits well with the already mentioned propensity of the native inhabitants here to venerate divinities of specific locales or peoples. The cult of such tutelary deities did not only translate into the Roman Lares and Lares Viales, but also appears to have resided under various dedications to Tutela and the Genius. We have seen that these deities sometimes received native epithets. It is thus likely that Tutela Bolgensis, Berisus and Tiriensis were in essence invocations of local protector divinities (Nos.24,25,35, Cat.III). This may well also have been the case with a dedication set up Bloena, the daughter of Sabinus, for the Genius Castelli, and the various others listed previously (No.28, Cat.III).

In turning to invocations of classical tutelary divinities without epithets we must be careful and not be tempted to assume that all dedications to the various classical protective divinities in actuality reflect indigenous cult. For example, in the *Conventus Asturum* two dedications were made to the Genius of the Legio VII Gemina which likely hold no relation to native worship (Nos.201,202, Cat.II). Likewise, a dedication to the Genius Populi Romani from the *Conventus Bracaraugustanus* and another to the Genius Praetorii from Astorga reflect non-native veneration (Nos.17,233, Cat.II). It is not the purpose of this essay to suggest the Roman tutelary deities always acted as a façade for the veneration of similar indigenous divinities. All that can be said is that tutelary gods played a key role in native religion in north-west Hispania. This role appears to have come to be filled in many cases by such Roman equivalent divinities as the Lar, Lares, Lares Viales, Tutela and the Genius.

External Parallels
The prolific dedications to the Lares Viales were a phenomenon peculiar to the north-west of the Iberian Peninsula, though such dedications occurred on occasion in Cantabria and Celtiberia (Curchin 1991:159). That the more 'Romanized' areas of Hispania did not venerate such a cult has been taken as evidence of its indigenous nature (Bermejo Barrera 1978:77). That said, protective divinities are not wholly absent from the rest of Roman Spain. For example, Bandua, as noted previously, was adored on a patera from Cáceres which depicted her as Tyche-Fortuna (Blázquez 1983:295-6). This protective divinity was also venerated in Orgaz, Toledo (EE, Vol.8, no.179). Similarly, a stone inscription from the Castro de Tres Ríos (Viseu, Portugal) invoked the divinity 'Penticis,' whom Untermann believes to be a protector divinity of a specific family or clan (1965:11,12).

Tutelary and topical divinities are, furthermore, widely attested throughout the Celtic provinces, whether related to such places as springs and mountains (as we have seen in previous sections), or communities and peoples (Jufer & Luginbühl 2001:15). It is interesting to note, though, that in the case of southern Aquitania the Roman equivalents of native protector divinities, the Genius and Lares, are poorly attested according to Fabre (1992:182). The only such tutelary divinity to be favoured in the region was Tutela who, though present in north-west Hispania, is the least prolific of the classical protector deities in evidence there (Fabre 1992:182). This need not suggest that the area of the Pyrenees did not have a native religion oriented towards such protective divinities, but only that this aspect of their religion largely did not come to incorporate a classical façade. Considering that the greater majority of votive altars from this area were made to indigenous deities rather than classical, this seems all the more likely to have been the case (Rico 1997:303).

Also of note is the fact that, as in our area, many of the indigenous divinities recorded throughout the Empire appear on only one occurrence (Green 1986:32). This may again reflect their special relation to a certain community or peoples. In line with this we see the deity Brixia invoked at the Italian city bearing her name, as we also see Cemenelus adored in the ancient Gallic community of Cemenelum, and Aventia in Aventicum (modern Avenches) in Switzerland, to name only a few examples (CIL V 4202 & 7871; CIL XIII 05071-3; Jufer & Luginbühl 2001:88,89). Clearly a devotion to a protector divinity of the community or group was a high priority on the minds of many of the inhabitants of the Empire, just as it clearly was with the indigenous peoples of north-western Roman Spain.

Warrior Divinities

Like many indigenous peoples of the west of the Roman Empire, the inhabitants of north-western Hispania worshipped a warrior god. Evidence shows that such a bellicose divinity was venerated here before and throughout the Roman period. From Galicia and Lusitania come a number of pre-Roman age stone representations of warriors. These figures are often found headless, and either seated or standing. They hold a small circular shield and a short sword and on occasion they are adorned with torques (Santos Yanguas 1991:335; Savory 1968:251). These figures were mainly found positioned guarding the entrances to *castros* (Lenerz-de Wilde 1995:547). It is not only such archaeological evidence that suggests a warrior cult pre-dated the Roman period here. Ancient authors such as Strabo also make reference to it. He tells us that the northerners in Hispania sacrificed horses, goats and prisoners to a native equivalent of Ares (3.3.7). Herodotus also notes that these northerners did not erect statues, altars or temples to any of their gods save Mars (4,59). It is thus not surprising to find that worship of an indigenous warrior divinity permeated through into the Roman period.

With Roman domination and the subsequent introduction of epigraphic veneration, the native warrior god came to be known through various inscriptions in our area of interest. He often was invoked under the denomination 'Cosus,' or variants of this (Map 10) (Bermejo Barrera 1978:54). These dedications were found dispersed throughout all three *Conventus* of the north-west of Roman Spain. Six dedications to deities with names deriving from 'Cosus' were found in the *Conventus Lucensis,* eight in the *Conventus Asturum,* and three in the *Conventus Bracaraugustanus* (two of these with *Cor-* roots). It is worth noting, though, that a dedication to 'Cososus Deus Mars' which was once thought by many scholars to originate in Braga appears instead to hail from Levroux, near Bituriges Cubes in Gaul (M. Chastagnol in Disscussion in Lambrino 1965:240; Tranoy 1981:292; CIL II, p.706). Nevertheless the association between Mars and native Cosus is still made on this inscription, albeit in a different Roman province. Of course the epigraphic material is rarely clear and often lends itself to varying hypotheses. This is the case with another inscription to 'Coso M / Vegetianus Fus/cus...' (No.84, Cat.I) which has been interpreted by some as another inscription to Cosus Mars (ie. Blázquez 1975:57 & 1983:118; Bermejo Barrera 1978:54; Lambrino 1965:231-2). Others, such as Hübner who initially interpreted the inscription as linked to Mars, now see the 'M' as the dedicators first initial (CIL II 5071 & 5628). So are the perils of interpreting epigraphy and coming to a distinct impression of the nature of indigenous Cosus.

There are a few other hints that may help in this pursuit though. An inscription to Cossua Segidiaecus from Arlanza in the *Conventus Asturum* includes the root *segh-* or *seghi-* in its epithet, which signifies to 'conquer' or 'subjugate' and also appears in Celtic and Germanic as *seghos* meaning 'victory' (No.137, Cat.I) (Bermejo Barrera 1978:55). Other variants of Cosus beginning with *Cor-* are also thought to perhaps relate to a warrior deity. Blázquez suggests that such deity names as 'Coronus' which includes this root are similar to the Gallic deity Mars Corotiacus (CIL VII, 93, and in Britain, RIB 213) and thus may also have a warrior aspect (1983:280-1). This seems a bit of a stretch, and I think in the end it would be prudent to take the Cosus and Cor- dedications on a case by case basis, understanding that one deity may have had varying aspects and that the evidence, while suggesting a possible link between Cosus and Roman Mars, is far from definitive.

We need not be disheartened though. The evidence for a native warrior deity in the north-west of Hispania does not end with Cosus. An inscription from the village of Tuy, on the bank of the Miño River links Mars with native Cairiogiegus (or Cariecus) (No.20, Cat. III). With this taken into account, a dedication originally interpreted as to 'Macarius' has more recently been proposed to be 'Ma(rti) Cario(ciegus)' (No.38, Cat.I) (Olivares Pedreño 2000b:56). Another inscription from Refojos de Lima interpreted as 'Lari Cari[e]co' may in fact have been to 'Mar[ti] Cari[e]co' (No.7, Cat.III) (AE 1983:561; Olivares Pedreño 2000b:56). All three of these dedications issue from the same general region, in west-central *Conventus Bracaraugustanus,* an area with its centre around Viana de Castelo. A final dedication from this zone, from Santa Vaia do Rio de Minhos, to the deity 'Carus' is, according to Olivares Pedreño, a possible abbreviation for yet another invocation of 'Cariecus' (No.21, Cat.I) (2000b:57). Indigenous 'Cariecus,' thus, seems to have been the presiding warrior deity of this zone.

From Villadepalos (Carracedelo, León) in the *Conventus Asturum* an altar was dedicated to the native deity 'Bodus' (No.130, Cat.I). The root *Bod-* is a Celtic word which relates to Victory and, thus, could well signal a native warrior deity (Tranoy 1981:297; Blázquez 1983:281). Another such divinity may be one depicted with a horned helmet and outstretched, open-palmed hands, from the region of Lourizán, near the city of Pontevedra (Bouza Brey 1946:110,113,114). Two other altars found with this depiction were consecrated to the native divinity 'Vestius Aloneicus' leading Bouza Brey to conclude that this was likely to be the deity represented on the relief (Nos. 120 & 121, Cat.I) (1946:115). Between Vestius Aloneicus, Bodus, Cariecus or Mars Cariogiegus and the various Cosus deities we have ample verification of the persistence of adoration of native warrior deities in the Roman period. It now stands to be assessed whether, and to what degree, Roman divinities were fit into this cult.

Roman Equivalents?

There are twelve and one possible inscriptions to Mars, including double-named dedications, which have been found in the three *Conventus*. Six and one possible come from *Bracaraugustanus,* four from *Asturum*, one from *Lucense,* and one from an imprecise location in the north-west (see Map.11). Not all of these dedications can definitively be taken to conceal an indigenous warrior deity. An inscription to Mars Gravidus was set up by a procurator of *Asturum* as was another to Mars Sagatus (No.240 Cat.II & No.37 Cat.III). In *Lucense* a dedication was made to Mars Augustus (No.161, Cat.II). All three of these likely reflect purely classical cult. The others, though, may possibly be a continuation of the process of assimilating Mars with indigenous warrior deities which we saw in the case of Mars Cairiogiegus, and perhaps also occurred with the dedication to Mars Tarbucelis (Nos. 20 & 21 Cat.III).

An association between the indigenous warrior divinity and the bull has been frequently evidenced in the western empire. For example from the Pyrenees we find a bronze depiction of Mars who is represented holding a shield which depicts a bull, and wearing a three horned helmet (Blázquez 1983:263). In keeping with this idea, in our area of interest, from Espiňo (Capilla de S. Roque) comes an altar inscribed with the word 'Marti' and decorated with a bulls skull on one of the lateral faces (No.97 Cat.II) (Rodríguez Colemenero 1977:307). This clearly appears to be a dedication to a classical deity, in name, though under iconography related to indigenous warrior cult. In contrast, a patera from Carriça, Alvarelhos (Santo Tirso) depicts a warrior deity in classical guise, though the dedication is not addressed to classical Mars. In fact it is not clear to which deity it was intended. The inscription reads: 'S Arqui Cim L Saur v.s.l.m.' This in the past has been interpreted as venerating native 'Saur...,' though this now appears more correctly to be the dedicator (No.75, Cat.I) (Tranoy 1981:314). All the same, these preceding two examples indicate a clear blending of native and Roman ideas of the warrior deity in north-west Hispania.

External Parallels

Turning our attention outside of the north-west of Hispania, more evidence for a native warrior cult comes to light. The parallel between Cososus Mars of Gaul and Cosus of north-west Spain has already been mentioned. Gallic dedications to Segomo, Mars Segomo, and Segomanna are similarly reminiscent of the dedication to Cosus Segidiaecus found in Arlanza (Bierzo) (No.137, Cat.I) (CIL XIII 02846, 05340, 01675, 02532, AE 1906,33 & 1994,1224). All contain the aforementioned *Segh-* root relating to victory (Bermejo Barrera 1981:269).

Native warrior deities are found depicted with horned helmets, similar to that worn by the image of Vestius Aloneicus from Lourizán, from many locales in the western Empire. Native Mars figures with his horned helmet on a number of iconographic pieces from Maryport, Kirby (Underdale, Yorkshire) and Burgh by Sands in northern Britain, and from Caernarvonshire and London in southern Britain (Ross 1992:203-4). Of course our big-handed divinity from Lourizán admittedly wears no apparent armour apart from his helmet and so may not have been a warrior, though the similarity of his representation with these from Britain is notable nevertheless.

Non-militaristic aspects of Mars are commonly found emphasized elsewhere in the western Empire. For example, he acted in Lingons, Drioux (Gaul) as a domestic and beneficent divinity associated with water (Thevenot 1955:9). In the Pyrenees at the sanctuary of Sarrat de Peyra, at Loudenville, Mars is worshipped as a deity of the mountain and thermal springs (Fabre 1992:184). Among the Treveri, at Trier and Pommern in Germany, he was venerated as the healing and beneficent Mars Lenus (Wightman 1970:211-214,220). Similarly, he is worshipped with curative aspects in Britain under the denomination of Mars Nodons (Wheeler & Wheeler 1932:41). This said, in the north-west of Hispania on the whole, as pointed out by an analysis by Bermejo Barrera, indigenous Mars seems to have been above all else a warrior deity (apart from the dedication to Mars Tilenus, a mountain or protector divinity) (1981:268). He could then be taken more in line with a warlike indigenous Mars equally known to the rest of the Empire. The epithets often given this divinity help elucidate his bellicose character: Beladonnis (destructor); Mogelius (great/large); Caturix (lover/king of combat); Olludius (very powerful); Cobannus (killer); Bellado (exterminator); Adsmerius (dangerous/formidable) etc. (Van Andringa 2002:134; Bermejo Barrera 1981:269). Clearly, Mars was a popular choice of divinity for the indigenous populations of the north-west of Hispania as with various areas of the western Empire. To many of his worshippers he quite possibly represented in translated form the continuing adoration of an essentially native divinity.

Other Divinities

I have thus far presented various categories into which many of the native divinities worshipped in the north-west of Hispania appear to fall. The categories are by no means fully inclusive or rigid. They are only used as a template in this essay in order to sort through the bewildering array of indigenous divinities attested. The template also allows for a bottom-up framework in which Roman divinity adoptions may be viewed through the lens of the pre-existing indigenous religious structure. That said, there are still those examples, both native and Roman, that do not conveniently fit into this framework and which need mention. For example, nothing has been said of the dedications to Lugubus/Lucobus (Nos.104 &105, Cat.I). Although there are only two, such dedications are nonetheless significant as they relate to the cult of Lugus which was widespread throughout the Celtic world (Caridad Arias 1999:6). The community names of Lugdunum (Lyon) and Luguvalium (Carlisle) reflect the extensive worship of this cult as does the city of Lucas Augusti (modern Lugo de Llanera) in our area of interest (Green 1986:16; Mangas 1995:167). Lucobus' adoration in the north-west gives us an interesting glimpse at interaction between the indigenous peoples of the western Empire and this corner of Roman Spain.

Equally neglected in the analysis thus far are the Matres. These deities, while not well attested in the north-west of Hispania, were named on two dedications from the Spanish Meseta which venerate the 'Matres Gallaicae' and 'Brigaecium.' These inscriptions appear to relate the Matres to Gallaecia and the Asturian town of Brigaecium, respectively (Curchin 2004:172). This suggests that these divinities did in fact enjoy a following amongst the peoples of the north-west of the Peninsula.

An indigenous solar divinity is further suggested in our

area by an altar from the valley of Limia dedicated to Mocius, which also has inscribed on it 'Ara Sol(is)' (No.40, Cat.I) (Blázquez 1991:67). Such a reverence of the sun appears to have been a common feature of the religion of indigenous peoples of the western Empire before and during Roman times. This is testified, in one respect, by prolific iconographic depictions of the sun-disc, depicted as a spoked wheel (Green 1986:39). The deity Aernus may be yet another nature deity from north-western Iberia. Worshipped on three altars from the *Conventus Asturum* and one from the *Conventus Lucense,* he was, according to Rodríguez Colemenero, a divinity related to woods and vegetation (Nos.77,127-9,Cat.I) (1977:298). In tune with this idea is an altar to this deity from Castro de Avelâs, near Bragance which is decorated with vegetal imagery consisting of three palms which adorn a large band surmounted by two volutes and a fronton (No.129, Cat.I) (Tranoy 1981:296). Aernus included amongst his devotees the whole *Ordo Zoelae,* a group from the *Conventus Asturum* mentioned by Pliny (*NH,*III.3.28). Still a further indigenous divinity with something of a following in the north-west of Hispania was Verora/Veroca. Three inscriptions to her have been found, all from the city of Lucus Augusti (Nos.117-119, Cat.I). Another dedication to 'Virrore Vilaeco' from the same locale may venerate this divinity, as may two dedications which have been varyingly interpreted as to Aernus or Verora (Nos.77,122,129, Cat.I). Unfortunately it is difficult to determine the nature of this divinity. The deity-name may derive from the Indo-European *veros* = true, though this does little to explain the religious role of this god (Arias Vilas, Le Roux & Tranoy 1979:38). The other two divinities mentioned, though, appear to fit well into the nature oriented indigenous religion of this corner of the Iberian Peninsula.

Roman Equivalents?
As with the native divinities there are those Roman deities who were attested in the north-west of Hispania but who have yet to be brought to light. The Roman gods for whom we have the greatest numbers of inscriptions, namely Jupiter, the Nymphs, Lares, Lares Viales, Genius, and Mars have all been discussed through the lens of their native equivalents (with the obvious caveat that not all examples relate to indigenous religion). After these divinities in frequency of dedications come Fortuna, Mercury, Diana and Tutela. Fortuna and Tutela were mentioned in the sections on aquatic and protective divinities. Mercury, though, requires mention. He was named on ten inscriptions, or 4% of all epigraphic texts venerating Roman deities. Four of these came from the *Conventus Lucense,* four from *Conventus Bracaraugustanus,* and two from *Conventus Asturum* (Nos.100-102, 162-165, 241, 242, Cat.II & No.5, Cat.III). He was only once found with an indigenous epithet, as 'Hermes Devoris' (Cat. III, No.5). Evidence of native worship of Mercury, though, is frequently found elsewhere in the Empire. This is important as it sheds light on a possible similar indigenous nature inherent in our Mercury dedications, and will be brought up in the subsequent section. Also, apart from a dedication by a procurator from León, none of the dedications to Mercury were set up by officials or military personnel, or even dedicators with *tria-nomina*. Only this aforementioned dedication from León and another from Braga were located in non-rural areas (Nos.102 & 242, Cat.II). Mercury, furthermore, is known within the Empire to have been equated with Celtic Lugus (Caridad Arias 1999:169). As this native deity was manifest in our area of interest it may be possible that a number of the dedications to Mercury were a continuation of this indigenous cult. There, therefore, may well be a dimension of native cult intrinsic in the Mercury dedications from our area of interest.

Diana is a further Roman divinity attested in our region who merits our attention. Though not eclipsing such prolific divinities as Jupiter and the Nymphs in the region she all the same was adored on eight inscriptions, or 3 % of all dedications to Roman gods (Nos.6,7,8,125,126,190-192, Cat.II). It is more difficult to see the indigenous milieu inherent in her veneration, though she again is known to have been assimilated with indigenous religion elsewhere in the Empire. Of her eight invocations three were set up by military personnel in the *Conventus Asturum* (Nos.190,191,192, Cat.II). It would seem likely that these dedications relate exclusively to the Roman cult of Diana. A few others such as that to 'Deane' or that to 'Diianii' from the *Conventus Bracaraugustanus* were accomplished in rural areas and have a distinctly local feel (Nos.6,7, Cat.II). Unfortunately the evidence is not in anyway conclusive enough to allow for an assertion that the cult of Diana concealed indigenous religious worship in our corner of the Iberian Peninsula.

In the case of Cybele who was attested on three dedications, we may assume foreign cult, and not native, to be inherent (Nos.3,4,124, Cat.II). According to Tovar and Blázquez, this divinity was brought to the north-west by oriental slaves from southern Lusitania and due to trade between Lisbon and Mérida and the Orient (1975:173). Various other Roman, Greek and Oriental divinities appear on one or two occasions in our area of interest. These may well relate directly to non-native cult, but they do not make up a substantial enough proportion of the epigraphic record to warrant an analysis at this point.

External Parallels
Some indigenous divinities that found only limited representation in our area such as the Lugoves and Matres were met with wider appreciation elsewhere in the Roman world. That the cult of Lugus spread widely throughout the western Empire has already been mentioned. The Matres, too, had great appeal to indigenous peoples. For example, Curchin records twelve inscriptions from the northern Meseta which invoked these female divinities and Webster records them as the 'most popular and widespread Celtic deities' in Britain (Curchin 2004:172; Webster 1986:63).

Turning to the Roman side, Mercury, who found fairly prolific devotion in the north-west of Roman Spain also did so elsewhere in the Empire. Caesar tells us that a native divinity in Gaul, whom he translates as Mercury, was most venerated by the peoples of that land (BG VI,17). In fact, in Jufer and Luginbühl's recent catalogue of divinities attested in the Celtic world, '*Répertoire des Dieux Gaulois,*' Mercury figures on 78 occasions double-named with an indigenous counterpart, from as wide-ranging locales as the three Gauls, Germany, Britain and the Danube provinces (2001:91-3). He even comes in Roman times to be coupled with native Rosmerta signaling a thorough blending of religious traditions (Webster 1986:58). The cult of Diana too mixed well with indigenous religion as is attested, for example, by two altars from the Pyrenees: one from Chaum which venerated her along with native Gar and Horolat and another from Ferrère which worshipped her and Montes (CIL XIII 60,382; Rico 1997:308). Such evidence for the association of Diana and Mercury with native cult elsewhere in the Empire helps strengthen the idea that our north-western Hispanic dedications may have relevance to the indigenous religious sphere also.

Sanctuary Sites

Many of the aforementioned divinities, through an analysis of their names or the placement of the altars dedicated to them, betray the locales in which they were worshipped. Having seen how intertwined the persistent ancestral religion was with all things natural it is fitting to assume much of this worship would have taken place outdoors. Thus we find the previously mentioned sanctuary to the protector/mountain divinity Lariberus Breus on the Monte Facho, and the sanctuary of Nabia created around a spring in the area of Braga. In order, then, to have a holistic understanding of the nature of indigenous religion in this region in the Roman period it would seem prudent at this point to bring to light what evidence we have for such places of reverence. A number of open air, rock sanctuary sites have been recorded in the area, most recently and thoroughly by Rodríguez Colmenero (1993), which give us a great insight into native patterns of religious veneration. Many of these do not include epigraphy and thus, whether cult practices went on in these places for generations or only on a few occasions, is difficult to infer (Alarcâo 1988, Vol.I:97). Nevertheless, some headway can be made towards this end due to a few exceptional sites which help elucidate the nature of the others.

One rock sanctuary that has acted as a model for the interpretation of many others is the famous site of Panóias, in the Council of Vila Real de Tras-os-Montes, first recorded by Jerónimo Contador de Argote in 1722 (Blázquez 2001:200). The epigraphy of this site has proven invaluable to the understanding of local ritual practices. The site consists of three rock outcrops from which stairs were hewn as were various rectangular hollows on the tops of the large rocks (Keay 1988:162). It can not be told how long this site was used for ritual activity. What is known, thanks to the engraved dedications of one prolific benefactor, G.C. Calpurnius Rufinus, is that it was in use in the Roman period and included the synchronized worship of various divinities. Five inscriptions were made here, four of which were set up by this same *legatus iuridicus* (Nos.9-12, Cat.II) (Alarcâo 1988, Vol.II:1/386). These inscriptions venerate a combination of numina, all gods and goddesses, unnamed gods, numina of the *Lapitae,* along with Oriental Serapis, Destiny and the Mysteries and the *Dei Severi* (or alternatively the Manes if we accept the conjecture of Rodríguez Colemenero) (Blázquez 2001:200-202; Alarcâo 1988, Vol.II:1/386; Rodríguez Colmenero 1993:61-71). Not only is this overwhelming blend of divinities of interest here, but also are the inscribed instructions for ritual included in the epigraphic texts.

From the inscriptions we can discern that victims at the site were sacrificed within a temple structure, *hic immolantur.* The inscription which makes reference to this temple may either suggest that Calpurnius Rufinus dedicated a temple with a *lacus* within, or that the *lacus* was dedicated by him within a pre-existing temple structure (Rodríguez Colmenero 1993:63-4). We also can deduce that the entrails of the victims were burnt in the *quadrata,* located nearby. The sacrificial blood would have flowed into the *laciculis* (Blázquez 1983:233-4; Keay 1988:162).

Yet one further inscription from nearby this site warrants our attention. This inscription appears in the area of the extended sacred group, within the village of Valnogueiras (Rodríguez Colmenero 1993:71). Previously taken to be a dedication to Jupiter Optimus Maximus Rurifebus, on careful re-examination of this Rodríguez Colmenero now tentatively suggests it in fact venerates a native divinity called 'Dumicebus' (No.32, Cat.I). The rock on which this dedication is inscribed also has a sacrificial hollow carved into it (Rodríguez Colmenero 1993:71). The thorough blending of religious worship at this site is only heightened by this invocation of an indigenous divinity. Here, therefore, in an evidently indigenous style sanctuary site, which was decorated with indigenous imagery and which invoked native divinities, Roman and Oriental gods came to be venerated alongside ancestral divinities.

If we have any doubt of the indigenous nature of this sanctuary site there are many other parallel examples from the north-west of the Iberian Peninsula that help assure us of this. The Pena Escrita sanctuary, mentioned in the section on mountain cult, was similar in design to that of Panóias. Though its epigraphy is difficult to discern its close proximity to altars revering Laroucus and Jupiter suggests it may have been a cult place of the divinity of the nearby Larouco Mountain (Rodríguez Colmenero 1993:75-6). Similarly, at Pilón de Mougás (Oya, Pontevedra) a rock sanctuary was discovered in

1896, on the side of a mountain facing the ocean. A great basin, today in the Museum of Pontevedra, was cut out of a large block of granite, 2.75 by 1.35m (Rodríguez Colmenero 1993:93-4). Following the interpretation of Rodríguez Colmenero, an inscription here tells us that the basin was for the victims of Silius Eorinus, an otherwise unknown native divinity (1993:95). These two examples, then, shed further light on native sacrificial practices and worship in this corner of the Iberian Peninsula.

This is again elucidated by a number of similar, though anepigraphic, rock sanctuary sites. At Paredes (Leiro) there was a rock sanctuary akin to that of Panóias in appearance, which also contained a depression for the cremation of sacrificial victims (Blázquez 1983:229). Some other sites consisting of such elements as rock-cut stairs, niches or hollows, and canals, all relating to ritual activity, are known from: Esponde (Ribadavia), Oímbra (Verín), Canzaba (Mazeda), Alfériz (Chaves), Castor de Novás, Pía de Santa (Abaríz), Fonte de Lagarto (Cameixa, Bobalás), and possibly Ourantes (Barbantes), among others (Blázquez 1983:229-230; Tranoy 1981:281). Such sanctuaries fit well into a belief in the divinity of nature which seems to have been held by the indigenous peoples of north-western Iberia throughout the Roman period.

Another possible native sanctuary site worth mention includes a large rock with two inscriptions to Cosunae and Munidi, found in Sanfins, Eriz, Paços de Ferreira (Nos.25 & 43, Cat.I). The second inscription has been varyingly interpreted as to 'Numinib(us),' 'Nimidi Fiduenearum' and most recently 'Munidi Fiduene' (Leite de Vasconcelos 1905:188-9 & CIL II 5607; Marco Simón 1992-3:323; Rodríguez Colmenero 1993:80). Marco Simón notes that the 'Fiduenearum' epithet of the second inscription includes the radical *vidu-* which is a Celtic term for a wood or forest. He also notes that this rock inscription is located in close proximity to the ancient community of Nemetobriga (1992-3:323). A Celtic 'nemeton' was an open air sanctuary where exchange between the divine and human worlds took place (Marco Simón 1992-3:318). Thus, Nemetobriga may have been a community of/or near a sacred clearing. This 'nemeton' could then have been the site of our rock inscription. Be this as it may, what is clear is that here, as in the other examples listed, indigenous divinities were being worshipped in an open air environment, in a manner characteristic of the native religion.

Conclusion

This essay has attempted to isolate the nature of indigenous worship in the north-west of Roman Spain and establish to what degree it altered during the period of Roman domination. Through the various sections of this paper we have seen that the inhabitants of the *Conventus Bracaraugustanus, Asturum* and *Lucense* worshipped a bewildering array of different divinities. That over half of the native divinities attested from our region were only recorded on one occasion suggests a religion quite different from the formalized Roman pantheon. Clearly the divinities of the north-west of Iberia were most often intimately linked to certain peoples, places or topographical phenomenon. We, hence, need not have been surprised to note a proliferation of dedications to such Roman tutelary deities as the Lar, Lares, Lares Viales, Genius, and Tutela. This appears not as a paradigm shift, but as a continuation of an established pattern of religious worship under a new denomination.

In the same vein many natural phenomena were adored in the indigenous religion of the area. As numerous mountain chains shaped the topography of this corner of the Iberian Peninsula, and as these chains were a common locale for the native communities, or 'castro' settlements, it is not altogether unforeseen for an indigenous worship of high places to have been manifest in the region. Sacred peaks were thus invoked under the name of the mountain in question, or as the wide-spread native god Reve. Jupiter, the great Roman celestial god, would then have been an obvious choice for continuation of this cult under the terminology of the new rulers. Jupiter not only was associated with native mountain worship in north-west Iberia, but also appears elsewhere in the western Empire in this role. An example of this was mentioned from the Pyrenees and another from the region of the Alps. Of course, Jupiter clearly cannot be taken to conceal a native mountain divinity in all of his 117 dedications. Those set up in high places though, with non-official dedicators, may well be taken to form part of this ancestral cult.

As local devotion to divinities of high places appears to have continued throughout the Roman period so too, it seems, did indigenous veneration of aquatic phenomena. This realm of worship is typified by the widely attested divinity Navia/Nabia who appears to have been related to various waters. She was the goddess venerated at the sacred spring of the Fonte do Idolo as well as in Marecos as Navia Corona, a protector nymph of the Danigi (Blázquez 1962:178; Alarcâo 1988, Vols.I & II: 93, 1/457). Other native divinities such as Coventina, Bormanicus, Tameobrigus, Edovius, Suldis..., and Durius appear equally to have been deities associated with water cult. All this understood, we once again need not be surprised when we turn to the epigraphic record of Roman deities and see that the Nymphs commanded a great following in our region. They appear on their own and with native epithets in all three of the north-western *Conventus* and clearly mark yet another example of endurance of local cult.

In attempting to isolate trends of indigenous religion in the north-west of Hispania I also noted that a native warrior cult appears to have prevailed through from pre-Roman into Roman times, and quite likely was adapted to be worshipped under its Roman equivalent. The dedications to Vestius Aloneicus, Bodus, Cariecus or

Mars Cariogiegus and the numerous invocations of Cosus in all their varied spellings, were recorded as possible evidence for such a native cult. This cult may have been reflected prior to Roman times through the erection of warrior statues, or 'guerreros,' common to southern *Conventus Bracaraugustanus*. Then, in Roman times the locals appear to have continued in their worship of a bellicose divinity though now occasionally under the denomination of classical Mars.

It is not only through various votive altars that we may note a persistence of indigenous religion in the north-west of Iberia during the Roman period. The various aforementioned rock sanctuaries also provide evidence of this. Unfortunately, it is difficult to know precisely whether such sites had a long duration before the Roman period, though hopefully further archaeological recovery in the future will shed light on this question. These rock sanctuaries, nevertheless, fit well into what we know of the nature-based indigenous religion of our region. They range from those such as Panóias where a thorough blending of religious traditions was apparent to other sites, purely indigenous in character and often without Latin epigraphy.

It appears, therefore, that the indigenous religion of the north-west of Hispania persisted with great vitality in the Roman period. This is not to say that the natives of this corner of the Peninsula were in any way opposed to the adoption of Roman cultural forms as was attested in Jane Webster's view of 'Romanization.' In contrast, they not only adopted their conquerors habit of dedicating votive inscriptions to the gods, they also on many occasions adopted the Roman gods into their own worship. Again, this analysis falls into the trap, mentioned by James, in which the elite may be given too much agency in this process. It is very difficult to deduce whether those without the means to adopt such Roman cultural forms as the votive altar in fact adopted aspects or denominations of this religion all the same, and this realm unfortunately must remain largely shrouded in mystery. What is of importance here, though, is the qualification that those natives who did openly adopt Roman deities and left evidence of this, did so selectively to fit their already established patterns of worship. Under whichever divinity it came to be worshipped a mountain, stream, river or spring could still hold the same sacred significance to the north-western Iberian inhabitants in Roman as in pre-Roman times. Deities, be they called by the name Bandua, Tutela or some other denomination, were invoked to protect the land, the people and their communities. Thus, Romanization in north-west Hispania seems to have been a process of cultural synthesis fuelled by both Roman introductions of their cultural forms and elite native desire to assimilate these aspects. In the realm of religion this process, though, appears to have largely been exercised on the terms of the local inhabitants of the region. That is, they selectively adopted forms of their conqueror's religion to fit their pre-existing patterns of worship. The essence of their religion, then, was little affected by the introduction of their conqueror's gods.

Catalogue I
Inscriptions to Indigenous Deites
Conventus Bracaraugustanus

1. Abna
   - 'Fuscinus Fusci d(eae) d(ominae) a(ugustae?) Abne(=Abnae) m(erito) l(ibens) a(nimo) p(osuit)' (Encarnação 1975:78). The 'D.D.N. Abna,' is suggested by Tranoy (1981:268) to be 'deux(a) dominus(a) noster(ra) Abna.'
   - Location = S.Martinho do Campo (S. Tirso).
   - Dedicator = Fuscinus
   - References = Tranoy 1981:268; Blázquez 1962:219; Encarnação 1975: 78; ILER 704.

2. Albocelus
   - 'Albocelo' (ILER 716). Inscription is now lost.
   - Location = Vilar de Maçada (Vila Real)
   - Dedicator = Unsure
   - References = Tranoy 1981:269; CIL II 2394; Blázquez 1962:71; ILER 716

3. Ambiorebis
   - 'Ambi/orebi / [A]rquius / [C]antab[r(i)] / l(ibens) a(nimo) p(osuit)' (Le Roux & Tranoy 1973:201).
   - Location= Braga
   - Dedicator = Arquius the son of Cantaber
   - References = Tranoy 1981:269; Le Roux & A.Tranoy 1973: 201; AE 1973, 308.

4. Ameipicrius/Ambieicer
   - 'Ampeipicri / sacrum / A(ulus) Crassius / Paternus / v(otum) s(oluit) l(ibens) l(aetus)' (Blázquez 1962:169). Tranoy has 'Ambiecer' (1981:269). Leite de Vasconcelos has 'Ameipicrius' like Blázquez, but has the dedicator as 'A. Crassicius Paternus' (1905:333). ILER 717 has 'Ameipicri' as the deity and 'A(ulus) Crasicius Paternus' as the deicator.
   - Location = Braga
   - Dedicator = A. Caecicius Paternus
   - References = Blázquez 1962:169; Tranoy 1981:269; Liete de Vasconcelos 1905:333; ILER 717.

5. Ariounae Minocesgaigae
   - 'Ariounis / Minocesg/aigis / (Caius) Narcisius / Rufus / v(otum) s(oluit) l(ibens) m(erito)' (AE 1990, 540).
   - Location = Sto. Tomé de Nocelo, Sobreganade, Porqueira.
   - Dedicator = (Caius) Narcisius Rufus
   - References = AE 1990, 540.

6. Bandua
   - 'Deo Vexillor(um) / Martis Socio / Banduae' (IRG IV, 87).
   - Location = San Pedro de Rairiz de Veiga
   - Dedicator = Unsure
   - References = CIL II 215; IRG IV, 87.

7. Bandua
   - 'Bandu/e Corn/elius O/culatu/s v.s.l.m' (CIL II 2498).
   - Location = Cova de Lua (Espinhosela, Bragance)
   - Dedicator = Cornelius Oculatus
   - References = Tranoy 1981:279; CIL II 2498 Blázquez 1962:55; Encarnação 1975:140; Leite de Vasconcelos 1905: 337; ILER 757.

8. Bandua Aetobricus
   - '……cius / Cluti? f(ilius) Ba/ndue Ae/tobrico / v(otum) [l(ibens)] a(nimo) s(oluit)' (IRG IV, 86). In Tranoy, 'Bandua Aetobrigus,' (1981:279). In CIL 2515, 'Bandueatobrigus.'
   - Location = Codosedo (Sarreaus)
   - Dedicator = Unsure.
   - References = Tranoy 1981:279; CIL II 2515; IRG, IV, 86; Blázquez 1962:58-9.

9. Bandua Calaigus
   - 'Bandue / Cal[ai?]go / Tere[nti]a / Rufina / v(otum) l(ibens) m(erito) s(oluit)' (IRG IV, 88). AE 1987, 562m has 'Bandue / Cadogo' instead.
   - Location = Mixos (Verín).
   - Dedicator = Terentia Rufina (Roman name) (Tranoy 1981:266).
   - References = Tranoy 1981:279; IRG IV 88; Blázquez 1962:59; Rodríguez Colmenero 1977:313; AE 1987, 562m; ILER 758.

10. Bandua Lansbrica
    - 'Bandua Lansbricae Aemilius Reburrinus' (HE 1989, no.492). Also, 'Bandu/a Ianoe/lica Fae/nirusas / aram v(otum) s(oluit)' (IRG IV, 89). To 'Bandua Lanobrica' in Tranoy (1981:280).
    - Location = Eiras (San Amaro, Orense).
    - Dedicator = Aemilius Reburrinus
    - References = HE 1989, no.492; Tranoy 1981:280; IRG, IV, 89; AE 1974, 408.

11. Banda Raeicus/ Banderaeicus
    - 'Atlus / Raeburri / fil. Band/eraeico / v.s.l.m' (ILER 750). Tranoy has 'Banda Raeicus' (1981:279).
    - Location = Ribeira da Pena (Vila Real), (Now lost).
    - Dedicator = Atlus/Attus, son of Raeburrus.
    - References = CIL II 2387; Blázquez 1962:51; Tranoy 1981:279; Encarnação 1975:126-8; Leite de Vasconcelos 1905:337; ILER, 750.

12. Bandua Veigebreaecus
    - 'v(otum) s(oluit) l(ibens) m(erito) / Bandue / Veigebra/eaego / M(arcus) Siloni/us Gal(eria) Si/lanus / sig(nifer) coh(ortis) I/ Gall(icae) C(ivium) R(omanorum)' (IRG IV, 85). Rodríguez Colmenero has 'Velgebreagus' (1977:312).
    - Location = Rairiz de Veiga (Ginzo de Limia).
    - Dedicator = M. Silonius Silanus (Roman tria-nomina), a soldier of the Cohors I Gallica civium Romanorum.
    - References = Tranoy 1981:280; Blázquez 1962:59-60; IRG IV, 85; Rodríguez Colmenero 1977: 312; ILER, 762.

13. Bandua Virubricus
    - 'Bandu(ea) V/irubrico / Mont(ius?) Mo[n]/tanus Co/nsacra (vit) ex voto' (IRG IV, no.84). Also as: 'Bandua Verubrigus' (Tranoy 1981:280) and 'Banduaerubricus' (Blázquez 1962:57-8).
    - Location = Arcuelos (Retorta, Laza, Verín).
    - Dedicator = Montius Montanus
    - References = Tranoy 1981:280; Blázquez 1962:57-8; IRG IV 84; ILER 759.

14. Bandua Vordeaecus
    - 'Bandu / Vorde/aeco sac/rum Sul/picius Pa/ternus v[o]/tum solui[t]' (AE 1991, 1039).
    - Location = Seixo de Anciâes, Carrazeda, Bragance.

- Dedicator = Sulpicius Paternus
- References = AE 1991, 1039.

15. Bormanicus
- 'Medam/us Camal / Bormani/co v.s.l.(m)' (CIL II 2402). Leite de Vasconcelos has 'Camali (filius)' rather than 'Camal' (1905:269).
- Location = Caldas de Vizuela
- Dedicator = Medamus, son of Camalus
- References: Tranoy 1981:269-70; CIL II 2402; Blázquez 1962:172; Leite de Vasconcelos 1905:269; ILER 768.

16. Bormanicus
- 'C. Pompeius Gal(eria) Caturonis f(ilius) Rectugenus Uxsamensis Deo Bormanico v(otum) s(oluit) p(ecunia) [s(ua)?]. Quisquis honorem agitas, ita te tua Gloria seruet, praecipias puero ne linat hunc lapidem' (CIL II 2403). Leite de Vasconcelos has 'M(ot)ugenus' instead of 'Rectugenus' (1905:268).
- Location = Caldas de Vizuela
- Dedicator = C. Pompeius Galeria son of Caturnus in CIL II 2403. As: C. Pompeius Mo…genus (?) Caturonis f(ilius) in Tranoy (1981:269-70).
- References = CIL II 2403; Blázquez 1962:171; Leite de Vasconcelos 1905:268; ILER 769.

17. Caepol….? and the Genius of the Conventus Bracaraugustorum?
- '[---]Caepol[-- et Genius] / Conv[entus Bracaraug(ustorum)] / Ti(berius) Claudi[us Claudianus praef(ectus)] / c(o)ho(rtis) Bra[car(um) Avgvst(anorum) statuam] / aurea[m dedit dedicauitqve]' (CIRG II, no.116). Only part of this monumental granite inscription remains (CIRG II, no.116).
- Location = Santa Eufemia de Tuy
- Dedicator = A soldier of a cohort, T. Claudius Claudianus, prefect of the cohortis
- Bracarum Augustanorum.
- References = Tranoy 1981:270; Blazquez 2001:178; CIRG II, no.116; IRG III, 30; CIL II 5613.

18. Calaicia / Calandia
- 'Calandiae / Rufus Fl/avi f. / s(erv.) f. c.' (ILER 5083b). 'Calaicia' in Tranoy (1981:271) and 'Galaicia[e]' in AE 1977, 446.
- Location = In front of the chapel of Santa Comba, in Sobreira (Paredes, Porto), grouped with another altar which was effaced (Tranoy 1981:271).
- Dedicator = Rufus the son of Flavus
- References = AE 1977, 446; Tranoy 1981:271; ILER 5083b.

19. Candeberonius Caeduradius
- 'Cand/ebero/nio Ca/edura/dio' (Le Roux & Tranoy 1973:198).
- Location = Braga (Vila Nova da Mares)
- Dedicator = Unknown
- References = Tranoy 1981:271; Le Roux & Tranoy 1973:198-99; AE 1973, 306.

20. Carius
- Cari(o) /De(o)/ Flac(c)us/ Secundi /v(otum) /s(oluit) (IRG IV, 97). Tranoy follows this interpretation, though Blázquez (1962:76) puts 'Cari…Beflacis,' and 'Cari..be' is used in CIL II 2531, IRG IV, 97 and ILER, 778.
- Location = San Juan de los Baños (Bande, Orense; near Limia).
- Dedicator = Secundus, son of Flaccus
- References = Tranoy 1981:271; CIL II, 2531; IRG IV,97; Blázquez 1962:76; ILER, 778.

21. Carus
- 'Caro / cons(acratum) / Q(uintus) P(osuit) M(erito)' (Blázquez 1962:209). The text is difficult to work out but is clearly dedicated to the native god Carus (Alarcâo 1988, Vol.II: 1/45)
- Location = Santa Vaia do Rio de Minhos, Arcos de Valdevez.
- Dedicator = Uncertain. Seems to be the initials Q.P.M.
- References = Tranoy 1981:271-2; Alarcâo 1988, Vol. II:1/45; Blázquez 1962:209; Leite de Vasconcelos 1905:336; ILER, 779.

22. Castaeci (or ae)
- 'Rebur/rinus / lapida/rius Ca/staecis / v.l.(s)/ m' (CIL II 2404).
- Location = Santa Eulália de Barrosas (Lousada), between S. Miguel das Caldas and S. Adriâo Pereira Caldas.
- Dedicator = The stone-cutter Reburrinus
- References = Tranoy 1981: 272; CIL II, 2404; Blázquez 1962:173; Leite de Vasconcelos 1905:190-1; ILER, 780.

23. Coronus
- 'Corono' (inscribed on the side of the altar) and 'Patern/us Flav / ara pos/uit iixs v/oto mii/rito / volii' (CIL II 5562).
- Location = The region of Crasto (Cerzedelo, Guimarâes).
- Dedicator = Paternus, son of Flavus
- References = Tranoy 1981:273; CIL II 5562; Blázquez 1962:117; Encarnação 1975:160-2; Leite de Vasconcelos 1905:331-3; ILER 787.

24. Coru…?
- 'Coru-/abe / Medamus / Camali' (CIL II 5594). Inscribed on a rock.
- Location = Briteiros
- Dedicator = Medamus, son of Camalus
- References = Tranoy 1981: 273; CIL II 5594; Blázquez 1962:117; Encarnação 1975:162-3.

25. Cosunea
- 'Cosuneae/ F(iduene) s(oluit) (votum)' (Rodríguez Colmenero 1993:80). Along with another inscription to 'Munidi Fiduene' (or 'Numidi Fiduenearum') on a granite outcrop (see No.43, Cat.I) (Alarcâo 1988:97).
- Location = Sanfins (Eiriz, Paços de Ferreira)
- Dedicator = Unknown
- References = Rodríguez Colmenero 1993:78-81; Alarcâo 1988:Vol.I, 97 & Vol.II, 1/370; Tranoy 1981: 273; CIL II 5607; Blázquez 1962:120; Leite de Vasconcelos 1905:188-9; Encarnação 1975:169-171.

26. Crougintoudadigo
- 'Crougin/touda/digoe / Rufonia / Sever(a)' (CIRG II, no.91).
- Location = Mosteiro de Ribeira (Ginzo de Limia).
- Dedicator = Rufonia Severa
- References = CIRG II, no.91; CIL II 2565; IRG IV 91; Blázquez 1962:77; Tranoy 1981:274; ILER 795.

27. Cusenemeoecus

- 'deo d/omen/o Cusuneneo/eco ex / voto // Seve/rus p/osuit' (ILER 796). See also twin dedication to Neneoecus (No.51, Cat.I).
- Location = The concelho of Santa Tirso (Porto).
- Dedicator = Severus
- References = CIL II 5552; Tranoy 1981:274; Blázquez 1962:121; Leite de Vasconcelos 1905:326-7; ILER 796.

28. Dadruuilus (or Madruuilus)
- 'Dadruuilo (or Madruuilo) / [---/---/---] Iuliu/s Nelii v(otum) s(oluit) l(ibens) m(erito)' (AE 1983, 562e).
- Location = Vilarelho da Raia, Chaves.
- Dedicator = Iulius, son of Nelius?
- References = AE 1983, 562e.

29. Daea Sancta
- 'Daeae / sancta[e] / sacrum / [A]nicius / […]' (AE 1983, 559).
- Location = Castro of São Lourenço (Vila Cha, Esposende).
- Dedicator = Anicius
- References = AE 1983, 559; Tranoy 1981:274.

30. Debaronus Mucaigaegus
- 'Debaro/ni Muce/aigaego / Fuscinus / Fusci f(ilius) / v(otum) l(ibens) a(nimo) s(oluit)' (AE 1983, 562g).
- Location = Aveledas, Chaves
- Dedicator = Fuscinus, son of Fuscus
- References = AE 1983, 562g.

31. Dioses Caulesisaeci
- 'D(iis) D(eabus) / Caulecisaec(is) / sacrum posit(um) / V(alerius) Fl(avus) dedicauit / pro salute sua et suorum' (IRG IV, 96).
- Location = Castro Caldelas
- Dedicator = Vlarius Flavus (?)
- References = IRG IV, 96; CIL II 2551.

32. Dumicebus
- 'Dumi/cebo/ T(itus) S(ulpicius) Pos(uit)' (Rodríguez Colmenero 1993:74). Though AE 1987, 562 has: '[I(ovi)] O(ptimo) M(aximo) / Ruro/febo (que) d(eo) / T(itus) S(ulpicius) Rufus / f(aciendum) c(urauit).' It is inscribed on a rock and very difficult to interpret.
- Location = Panóias (Assentos, Vale de Nogueira,Vila Real).
- Dedicator = Titus Sulpicius Rufus
- References = Rodríguez Colmenero 1993:71-4; AE 1987, 562.

33. Durbedicus
- 'Celea / Clouti / deo D/urbed/ico ex v/oto a. l.' (ILER 808).
- Location = Ronfe (Guimarães).
- Dedicator = Celea, daughter of Cloutius
- References = CIL II 5563; Blázquez 1962:174; Encarnação 1975:177-9; Tranoy 1981:274-5; Leite de Vasconcelos 1905:.329-331; ILER 808.

34. Durius
- 'Duri/ C Iulius / Pylades' (CIL II 2370).
- Location = Porto
- Dedicator = C. Iulius Pylades
- References = CIL II 2370; Blázquez 1962:174; Encarnação 1975:179-80; Tranoy 1981:275; Leite de Vaconcelos 1905:234; ILER 6567.

35. Laesus
- 'Elanicus Ta/urinus Lae/su vo. / l . sol' (Encarnação 1975:209).
- Location = Torre (Ousilhâo, Vinhais, Bragance) (Northeast Portugal).
- Dedicator = Elanicus Taurinus
- References = Tranoy 1981:275; Encarnação 1975:209.

36. Laraucus
- 'Larauc/o D(eo) Max(imo) P(ablius) F(ilius) D(ecio) Maxumo v(otum) l(ibens) a(nimo) s(oluit)' (Lourenço Fontes 1980:7). Or, Rodríguez Colmenero & Lourenço Fontes (1980:28): 'Larauco D(eo) Max(umo) Ped(roni) Maxumo v(otum) [l(ibente)] a(nimo) s(olvit).' AE 1980, 579 has 'Ped.' also.
- Location = Near the serra de Larauco, in the region of Montalegre, village of Vilar de Perdizes (Sanctuary called Pena Escrita).
- Dedicator = Either Pablius, son of Decius, or not apparent, depending on translation.
- References = Tranoy 1981:281; Lourenço Fontes 1980:7; Rodríguez Colmenero & Lourenço Fontes 1980:28; AE 1980, 579.

37. Larocus
- 'Larocu(i) / Ama Pitil(i)/i filia libii(s) / animo vo/tum riituli(t) / pro marito su(o)' (Le Roux & Tranoy 1973:211).
- Location = The village of Curral de Vacas, near Chaves
- Dedicator = Dedicated by Ama, daughter of Pitilius, for her husband
- References = Le Roux & Tranoy 1973:211; Tranoy 1981:281; AE 1973, 315; Rodríguez Colmenero 1977: 297.

38. Macarius
- 'Fron/tonian/us Fro/nton/is (filius) Ma/cari / v(otum) s(oluit) l(ibens) / m(erito)' (Blázquez 1962:69). Others interprets this as to 'Ma(rti) Cario(ceigo)' (1984:256) (Olivares Pedreño 2000b:56).
- Location = Lisouros (Paredes de Coura).
- Dedicator = Frontonianus, son of Fronto
- References = Tranoy 1981:275; Blázquez 1962:69; Olivares Pedreño 2000b:56; Encarnação 1975:230-1; ILER, 875.

39. • Maecus Rougiavesucus
- 'Deus Maeco Rougiavesucus or Maecorougiavesucus' (Tranoy 1981:275-6).
- Location = Igreja Minhotâes (Barcelos, Braga).
- Dedicator = Arcuius (indigenous name – Tranoy 1981:266)
- References = Tranoy 1981:275-6; Unpublished.

40. Mocius
- 'Ara Sol(is)' with a principal line: Iulia / Praenia / Mocion(i) v(otum) s(oluit)' (Rodríguez Colmenero 1977:296).
- Location = The Valley of Limia (Ginzo de Limia).
- Dedicator = Iulia Praenia
- References = CIL II 5621; Blázquez 1962:93; Tranoy 1981:276; IRG IV, 144; Rodríguez Colmenero 1977:296; ILER 882.

41. Moelius Mordoniecus
- 'Moeliso / Mordo/nieco / Caecili/us Fusc/us m(iles) le(gionis) V/II v(otum) s(oluit) l(ibens) m(erito)' (IRG IV, 92).
- Location = Cornoces, in the region of Orense.

- Dedicator = Caecilius Fuscus, a soldier of the Legio VII Gemina.
- References = Tranoy 1981:276; IRG IV, 92; ILER, 5997.

42. • Munidia
- 'Munidia' (Tranoy 1981:276-7).
- Location = Ribeirinha (Trêsminas, Vila Pouca de Aguiar).
- Dedicator = Q. Annius Modestus
- References = Tranoy 1981:276-7; Altar unpublished in the Seminaire de Vila Real.

43. Munidis (or Numinibus) Fiduene
- 'Munidi/Fiduene Aram / hic / l(ibens) [p(osuit)]' (Rodríguez Colmenero 1993:80). Leite de Vasconcelos has 'Numinib(us)' (1905:188-9). Along with another inscription to Cosunea on a granite outcrop (No.25, Cat.I).
- Location = Sanfins (Eiriz, Paços de Ferreira)
- Dedicator = Unknown
- References = Rodríguez Colmenero 1993:78-81; Alarcão 1988:Vol.I, 97 & Vol.II, 1/370; Tranoy 1981: 273; CIL II 5607; Blázquez 1962:120; Leite de Vasconcelos 1905:188-9; Encarnação 1975:169-171.

44. Mudia or Mundia
- 'Munide Ma[n]ius Varecrus ex vot(o)' (Encarnação 1975:238).
- Location = Chaves
- Dedicator = Manius Vacrecus
- References = Tranoy 1981:276-7; Encarnação 1975:237-40; ILER, 883.

45. Nabia
- 'Caturo Pintam(i) Nabiae [l]ibens [a(nimo) p(osuit)]' (CIL II 2378).
- Location = Monte Baltar between Porto and Penafiel (Vandoma, Paredes).
- Dedicator = Caturus, son of Pintamus
- References = Blázquez 1962:178; Tranoy 1981:281; CIL II 2378; Leite de Vasconcelos 1905:277; Encarnação 1975:240; ILER 894.

46. Nabia
- 'Nabiae / v(otum) s(oluit) l(ibens) a(nimo) / Rufinus Rebunius' (Parente 1980:132). 'Rubunius' in AE 1980, 581.
- Location = Covas (Trêsminas, Vila Pouca de Aguiar).
- Dedicator = Rufinus Rebunius
- References = Tranoy 1981:281; Parente 1980:132; AE 1980, 581.

47. Nabia
- 'Nabiae / Rufina / votum / s(oluit) l(ibens) m(erito)' (Blázquez 1962:178).
- Location = Fonte do Idolo, Braga.
- Dedicator = Rufina
- References = Blázquez 1962:178; Tranoy 1981:281; Encarnação 1975:242; ILER 886.

48. Nabia
- '…into / …ento / …i Lagi/us Na/biae v(otum) / s(oluit) l(ibens) m(erito)' (IRG IV, 80).
- Location = Mont de San Pedro (Nocelo da Pena, Ginzo de Limia).
- Dedicator = …Lagius?
- References = IRG IV 80; Tranoy 1981:281; CIL II 5622; ILER 895.

49. Nabia Corona (with Jupiter, (…)urgo, and Lida)
- 'O(ptimae) V(irgini) Co(nservatrici) or –rnigerae) et Nim(phae) Danigo / M Nabiae Coronae va/cca(m) bovem Nabiae agnu(m) / Iovi agnum / bove(m) la/ct(enem) [...]urgo agnu(m) Lidae cor(nigeram or –nutam) / ann(o) et dom(o) actum (ante diem) V (quantum) id(us) apr(iles) La/rgo et Mesallino co(n)s(ulibus) curator(ibus) / Lucretio Sab/ino postumo peregrino' (Tranoy 1981:282).
- Location = Marecos, near Penafiel (Porto).
- Dedicator = Unsure (Lucretius Vitulinus and Lucretius Sabinus Postumus Peregrinus are listed as the organizers of the sacrifice).
- References = Tranoy 1981:282-3; AE 1973, 319.

50. Nabiale Elaesurraecus
- '[N]abiale Elaesurraec(o) / sacrum / [p]ositum cura viccision(is)' (IRG IV, 81). Quintana Prieto (1969:37) has 'Abia…,' and CIL II 2524 has 'Abia Felaesurafro.' In ILER 5983 as 'Abiae Elaesurne.'
- Location = S. Juan de Camba (Castro Caldelas, Orense).
- Dedicator = Viccius Silo
- References = IRG IV, 81; Blázquez 1962:179; Tranoy 1981:282; Quintana Prieto 1969:37; CIL II 2524; ILER 5983..

51. Neneoecus
- 'Dom(ino) Deo / Neneoeco / Severu(s) / [S]aturni/ni f(ilius) vo/to posu/it numin(i)/…' (Blázquez 1962:122). See also twin dedication to Cusenemeoecus (No.27, Cat.I).
- Location = The concelho of Santa Tirso (Porto).
- Dedicator = Severus, son of Saturninus
- References = Blázquez 1962:122; Tranoy 1981:274; Encarnação 1975:164-9; ILER 896.

52. Ocaera
- 'Anicu/a Arqui / votum / libens / Ocaere / soluit' (CIL II 2458). ILER 903 has the dedicator as 'Anicius, son of Arquus.'
- Location = Serra de Gerêz, S. João do Campo, Terras de Bouro.
- Dedicator = Aniciua, son of Arquilius. Also the dedicator of altar to 'Daea Sancta' (No.29, Cat.I).
- References = Blázquez 1962:214; Tranoy 1981:277; CIL II 2458; Encarnação 1975:253-55; ILER 903.

53. Onimus Geius
- 'Onim(o) / Geio / G(aius) Iul(ius) / Seve/rinus / posuit' (AE 1987, 562j). It was earlier interpreted as 'O(ptimo) / I(ovi) M(aximo) / Geio / G(aius) Iul(ius) / Seve/rinu(s) / ex v(oto)' (AE 1981, 529). Tranoy also follows this latter reading (1981:302).
- Location = Servoy, Verín.
- Dedicator = G. Iuius Severinus
- References = AE 1987, 562j; AE 1981, 529; Tranoy 1981:302.

54. Proinetie
- 'Proinetie / Q(uintus) Apili/cus Se/veuer/us (sic) v(otum) s(oluit) l(ibens) m(erito)' (AE 1987:562h).
- Location = Ginzo de Limia, Orense
- Dedicator = Apilicus Seveuerus
- References = AE 1987:562h.

55. Reve
- 'Peregrinus / Apri f(ilius) Reve / eis v(oto)' (IRG IV, 93). Also, 'Reva Eistutus' or 'Reva Veistutus' in Tranoy

(1981:285), and 'Reve Eisuto' in Rodríguez Colmenero (1977:304-5).
- Location = Mosteiro de Ribeira (Ginzo de Limia)
- Dedicator = Peregrinus, son of Aper
- References = IRG IV 93; Rodríguez Colmenero 1977:304-5; Tranoy 1981:285; Blázquez 1962:184-5; ILER 913.

56. Reva (Ana Baraeco…?)
- 'Revva Ana / Baraeco…/ Afer Albini f(ilius) Turolus / v(otum) s(oluit) l(ibens) m(erito)' (IRG IV, 95).
- Location = Ruanes de Galicia (near Rubío, in Bande, Orense).
- Dedicator = Afer, son of Albinus and Turolus
- References = IRG IV, 95; CIL II 685.

57. Reva Laraucus
- 'D(eo) Reve/ Larauc(o) / Valliu(s) / Aper ex / vot(o)' (Rodríguez Colmenero & Lourenço Fontes 1980:27). In IRG IV, 94: 'Reve / Radauc/uae Liv…/ Aner… ex / voto.' A second illegible altar comes from the same site.
- Location = Baltar (Ginzo de Limia, Orense).
- Dedicator = Vallius Aper (Rodríguez Colmenero & Lourenço Fontes 1980:27), or Vale(r)ius Aper (Tranoy 1981:268). In IRG IV, 94: Liv… Aner…?
- References = Rodríguez Colmenero & Lourenço Fontes 1980:27; Tranoy 1981:281; IRG IV, 94; Rodríguez Colmenero 1977:305; AE 1976, 298.

58. • Reve Marandicuus
- 'Reve Marandicui' (Olivares Pedreño 2000:192). Villar has 'Reve Marandigui' (1994-5:247).
- Location = Guiâes (Vila-Real, near the Sierra de Marâo mountains).
- Dedicator = Pintamus
- References = Olivares Pedreño 2000a:192; Villar 1994-5:247-55.

59. Revve Reumiraecus
- 'Revve / Reumirae/co Fronto Vaucani f(ilius) v(otum) l(ibens) m(erito) s(oluit)' (Rodríguez Colmenero 1977:305). Tranoy has 'Revva Reumiragus' (1981:285-6).
- Location = Vilardevos (Florderrey Vello, Verín)
- Dedicator = Fronto, son of Vaucanus
- References = Rodríguez Colmenero 1977:305; Tranoy 1981:285-6.

60. Senaicus
- 'Sena/ico / Arquius / Cantabr(i) / l(ibens) a(nimo) p(osuit)' (Le Roux & Tranoy 1973:199).
- Location = Braga
- Dedicator = Arquius
- References = Tranoy 1981:269; Le Roux & Tranoy 1973:199-201; AE, 1973, 307.

61. Suldis …Antugaicis
- 'Suldis / …antu/gaicis / Flavinus / Flaus v(otum) s(oluit) l(ibens) m(erito)' (Rodríguez Colmenero 1977:309). To 'Suleae Nantugicae' (Tranoy 1981:277). Also proposed, to: 'Sulen Santu Gaicis' = IRG, IV, 98.
- Location = Condado (Padrenda, Orense).
- Dedicator = Flavinus, son of Flavus (Indigenous name).
- References = Rodríguez Colmenero 1977:309; Tranoy 1981:277; IRG IV, 98.

62. Tameobrigus
- 'Tameobrigo / Potitus / Cumeli / votum / patris / s.l.m' (CIL II 2377).
- Location = At the confluence of the Duoro and the Támega.
- Dedicator = Initially vowed by Cumelus, but erected by his son Potitus
- References = Tranoy 1981:277; CIL II 2371; Blázquez 1962:190; Leite de Vasconcelos1905:319-321; Encarnação 1975:276-80; ILER 931.

63. Tongenabiagus
- '[Cel]icus Fronto / Arcobricensis / Ambimocidus / fecit' and 'Tonge/nabiago' (ILER 938). CIL II 2419 has: 'Roncoe Nabiaco' as the deity. Blázquez (1962:194-6) and Tranoy (1981:283-5) have 'Tongoe' rather than 'Roncoe.'
- Location = Fonte do Idolo, Braga (on the rue do Raio, near the avenue of Maréchal Gomes da Costa, to the east of the ancient village).
- Dedicator = Caelius Fronto (of the city of Arcobriga, of the clan of Ambimogidi)
- References = Blázquez 1962:194-6; Tranoy 1981:283-5; CIL II 2419; Leite de Vasconcelos 1905:264-5; Encarnaçâo 1975:282-8; ILER 938.

64. Torius Gambictecus/Torolus Gombiciegus
- 'Torio / Gambic/teco Fla/vius Fla/vianus / v(otum) s(oluit) l(ibens) m(erito)' (AE 1973, 318). Tranoy has: 'Torolus Gombiciegus' as the deity name.
- Location = Pías (Orense) (Where it was found built into a modest chapel).
- Dedicator = Flavius Flavianus
- References = Tranoy 1981:278; AE 1973, 318.

65. Turiacus
- 'L. Valerius Silonus / miles . leg VI . Vict / Turiaco / v. s . l . m' (CIL II 5551).
- Location = Santo Tirso (Porto).
- Dedicator = L. Valerius Silvanus, soldier of the Legio VI Victix.
- References = Tranoy 1981:278; CIL II 5551; Blázquez 1962:196-7; Leite de Vasconcelos 1905:324-26; Encarnaçâo 1975:293-4; ILER 945.

66. Valmus/Valanis
- 'C. S. F./ Valmu(or an)/i v. l. s. p' (Le Roux & Tranoy 1973:214).
- Location = S. Pedro de Avioso (Maia).
- Dedicator = C.S.F.
- References = Le Roux &Tranoy 1973:214; Tranoy 1981:278.

67. Vibonus/Vironus
- 'Flaccus / Vibonis / l.v.v.i' (CIL II 2499).
- Location = Cova de Lua (Espinhosela, Bragance).
- Dedicator = Flaccus
- References = Tranoy 1981:278; CIL II 2499; Encarnação 1975:298.

Uncertain Readings from the Conventus Bracaraugustanus

68. • Aduana
- 'Aduana' or 'Apruna' (?). Inscription incomplete – large part of text disappeared (Tranoy 1981:268).
- Location = Trêsminas (Vila Pouca de Aguiar)
- Dedicator = Unsure
- References = Tranoy 1981:268.

69. Bandua Bricus
- '…/a Brico / Flaus A/pili Val/abricii/nsis vo/tum s l / m miirito (sic)' (Tranoy 1981:280). Deciphered here as to Bandua due to the –a at the end of the first word and the 'bricus' (/brigus) which is commonly associated with Bandua altars from the area. The altar is incomplete (Tranoy 1981:280).
- Location = Concelho de Villa Nova de Famalicâo, Caldas de Vizella.
- Dedicator = Flaus, son of Apilus
- References = Tranoy 1981:280; CIL II 5561.

70. D.S.K.G.L.LA.?
- 'D(omino or -ae) s(ancto or –ae) K( ) G( ) L( ) / Rufus / Rufini (filius) a(ram) / p(osuit) vo(tum) so(luit)' (AE 1983:564).
- Location = Giela (Arcos de Valdevez).
- Dedicator = Uncertain
- References = AE 1983:564; Tranoy 1981:272; Alarcâo 1988, Vol. II:1/48.

71. DO.SA.LA.LA?
- 'Do(mino or –ae) sa(ncto or –ae) / La( ) La( ) / a(ram) p(osuit) q(uod?) / vo(uit?) fr(ater) / Co(rnelia?) Rufila (sic) // (on the right) Soupi Camal(i) f(ilii)' (AE 1983:565).
- Location = Giela (Arcos de Valdevez).
- Dedicator = Uncertain
- References = AE 1983:158; Tranoy 1981:272; Alarcâo 1988, Vol. II:1/48.

72. …evus Vesterus
- '[…]iuo / Vestero / Val(eria) Rufa / ex voto / posuit' (AE 1983:563).
- Location = Alvarâes (Viana do Castelo)
- Dedicator = Valeria Rufa
- References = AE 1983:563; Tranoy 1981:278.

73. • …urgus
- '…urgus' (Tranoy 1981:278)
- Location = Marecos (Penafiel)
- Dedicator = Unsure.
- References = Tranoy 1981:266,278.

74. …eia…igus
- '…/…ia/….an/….igo/ pms/ ex v.' (Tranoy 1981:278)
- Location = Santa Eulalia de León (Vilamarín, Orense).
- Dedicator = P.M.S. (Tria-Nomina ?)
- References = Tranoy 1981:278; Unpublished.

75. Saur…?
- 'S. Arqui Cim. L. Saur. v.s.l.m' (Tranoy 1981:314).
- Location = Carriça, Alvarelhos, Santo Tirso
- Dedicator = S. Arqui Cim? Tranoy suggests 'S(extus) Arqui(us) Cim(bri) L(ibertus) Saur…' as the dedicator (1981:314).
- References = Tranoy 1981:314; CIL II 2373; Blázquez 1962:124.

76. …….vieania Ibanduicola
- '[…]/vieani[a or e]/bus Iban/duiocolis/ Corneli[a]/nus lib(ertus) / v(otum) s(oluit) l(ibens) m(erito)' (Le Roux & Tranoy 1973:212). AE 1973, 316 has: '[Matribus?] / Veiani[a or e]bus Ibanduicolis.'
- Location = Beiriz (Póvoa de Varzim)
- Dedicator = Cornelianus, a freedman
- References = Tranoy 1981:305; Le Roux &Tranoy 1973:212-13; AE 1973, 316.

Conventus Lucensis

77. Aernus
- 'Aer(no)/MV e(x) v(oto)/ h(anc) a(ram) s(oluit) [or s(acrauit)]' (CIRG II, no.33). Many attribute this altar to 'Verora' – IRG III,29; Blázquez 1962:217; ILER, 954. Tranoy believes it to be to 'Aernus' (1981:288).
- Location = Cangas, Pontevedra.
- Dedicator = Unsure
- References = CIRG II, no.33; IRG III,29; Blázquez 1962:217; Tranoy 1981:288; ILER, 954.

78. Anufeson(-)
- 'Au/su(a?) Ruf(i)/na d(e-) An/ufeson(-)/ a(ram) p(osuit)' (CIRG I, no.77).
- Location = Monte Dodro en Porto do Son (La Coruňa).
- Dedicator = Ausua Rufina
- References = CIRG I, no.77; Blazquez 2001:175; AE 1992, 1001.

79. Bandua
- 'Deo Ban[du(a)e] / Ti(berius) Cla(udius) Ci[-c.3-] / vo++ de[o sa]-/nto v(otum) / s(oluit) l(ibens) (merito)' (CIRG II, no.112).
- Location = In the farm, A Capela, Catoira.
- Dedicator = Tiberius Claudius Ci(?)
- References = CIRG II, no.112.

80. Bandua Boleccus
- 'Bandue B/olecco Suplicius / Sincerus C(?) / v(otum) s(oluit) l(ibens) m(erito)' (Arias Vilas, Le Roux & Tranoy 1979:no.56). The following translate the deity name as 'Banduso / Olecco': IRG II 20; Blázquez 1962:60-1; ILER 763.
- Location = Curbián (Palas de Rey, Lugo).
- Dedicator = Sulpicius Sincerus
- References = Tranoy 1981:288-9; Arias Vilas, Le Roux & Tranoy 1979:no.56; AE 1974, 388; IRG II 20; Blázquez 1962:60-1; ILER 763.

81. Cohventena
- 'Cohve/tene/ E r(esponso?) n(uminis?) (Arias Vilas, Le Roux & Tranoy 1979:no.57). As 'Coventinae' (IRG II, 22).
- Location = Os Curveiros (Friol, Lugo).
- Dedicator = Unknown
- References = Tranoy 1981:289; Arias Vilas, Le Roux & Tranoy 1979:no.57; IRG II, 22; Blázquez 1962:191.

82. Cuhue(tena?) Berralogecus
- 'Cuhve(tenae) / Berral/ogecu / ex voto / Flavius / Valeria/[n]u[s]…' (Arias Vilas, Le Roux & Tranoy 1979:no.58). IRG II, 21 and Blázquez 1962:191 have 'ocecus' and 'ocegus' respectively.
- Location = Santa Cruz de Lozo (Paradela, Lugo).
- Dedicator = Flavius Valerianus
- References = Arias Vilas, Le Roux & Tranoy 1979:no.58; IRG II, 21; Tranoy 1981:289; Blázquez 1962:191; ILER, 786.

83. • Coius Deus
- 'Coius Deus' (The 'i' may well be an 's' badly engraved) (Tranoy 1981:292).
- Location = Brandomil (Zas.).

- Dedicator = Mandania (The name in uncertain)
- References = Tranoy 1981:292.

84. Cosus
- 'Coso M / Vegetianus Fus/cus v s / [l m]' (Tranoy 1981:292). It is unclear whether the first M is an abbreviation of 'Marti' or the first initial of the dedicator (Tranoy 1981:292). Blázquez (1962:117-118; 1970:71) and Lambrino (1965:231) take the 'M' as 'M(arti).'
- Location = Brandomil (Zas.)
- Dedicator = (M) Vegetianus Fuscus.
- References = Tranoy 1981:292; CIRG I, no.39; IRG I, 7; CIL II 5628; Lambrino 1965:231; Blázquez 1962:117-118 and 1970:71; ILER 791.

85. Cosus Dominus
- 'Coso Do/mino Ae/b(ura) Ati (filia) Cil(ena) / exs vo/to p(osuit)' (CIRG I, no.22).
- Location = Logrosa (Negreira)
- Dedicator = Aebura, daughter of Atus, of the Cileni
- References = CIRG I, no.22; Blázquez 2001:175-6.

86. Cosus Oenaegus
- 'Coso / Oenae/go / G(aius) Iul(ius) / Nepos / ex vot(o)' (CIRG I, no.68). As 'Oenaecus' in Tranoy (1981:293).
- Location = S. Mamed de Seavia (Coristanco, La Coruña).
- Dedicator = C. Iulius Nepos
- References = CIRG I, no.68; Blázquez 2001:176; Blázquez 1962:118; Tranoy 1981:293; ILER 792.

87. Cosus Soagoecus
- '[D]eo Co/soe So/aegoe A/us Victo/[ri]s v(otum) s(oluit) l(ibens) m(erito)' (CIRG II, no.128). AE 1994, 959 agrees with this interpretation but Tranoy has: 'Deus Cosus Esoaecus' (1981:293).
- Location = Romani Vello (Portas, Caldas de Reyes)
- Dedicator = Aus - or - Flavus, son of Victor.
- References = CIRG II, no.128; Tranoy 1981:293; AE 1994, 959.

88. Cosus Udaviniagus
- 'Coso V/davini/ago / Q(uintus) V(---) L(---) / ex voto' (CIRG I, no.9). To 'Cosus Daviniagus' in Tranoy (1981:292) and 'Cosoudaviniagus' in Blázquez (1962:120).
- Location = The castro of Meiras (La Coruña)
- Dedicator = Abbreviated as Q.V.C.
- References = CIRG I, no.70; Tranoy 1981:292-3; Blázquez 1962:120; ILER, 794.

89. Dever …?
- 'Deo D/ever / ------' (CIRG II, no.119).
- Location = Found in 1972 in an excavation in the necropolis of San Vicente de O Grove (Cambados, Pontevedra), a fragment of this altar was built into the wall of the ruins of an ancient church, near the ocean (Tranoy 1981:289).
- Dedicator = Unknown
- References = CIRG II, no.119; Blázquez 2001:178; Tranoy 1981:289; AE 1977, 452.

90. Edovius
- 'Edovio / Adalus Clo/utai (filius) v(otum) s(oluit) l(ibens) m(erito)' (CIRG II, no.73).
- Location = Caldas de Reyes
- Dedicator = Adalus, son of Cloutaius

- References = CIRG II, no.73; Blázquez 2001:178 & 1962:175; Tranoy 1981:289; CIL II 2543; ILER, 811.

91. Lahus Paraliomegus
- ' Laho Par/aliomego / Caelius Ru/finus ex / (hedera) voto' (Arias Vilas, Le Roux & Tranoy 1979:no.5). As 'Iano Alioneco' in IRG II 12, and as 'Iano Par/alioneco' in Blázquez (1962:139), and corrected as 'Iaho Alioneco' in ILER 663.
- Location = Lugo
- Dedicator = Caelius Rufinus
- References = Tranoy 1981:289; Arias Vilas, Le Roux & Tranoy 1979:no.5; IRG II 12; Blázquez 1962:139; ILER 663.

92. Larius Breus Bro(s) Sancto
- 'Deo La/rio Bre/o Bro / [s]an(c)to' (CIRG II, no.1).
- Location = Sanctuary of Donón, (Hio, Pontevedra).
- Dedicator = Unknown
- References = CIRG II, no.1; Baños & Pereira-Menaut 1998:22; Blázquez 2001:177.

93. Lariberus Breus
- 'D[eo La]/ribe/ro Br/eo a/r(am) p(osuit) v(oto)' (CIRG II, no.2).
- Location = Sanctuary of Donón, (Hio, Pontevedra).
- Dedicator = Unknown
- References = CIRG II, no.2; Baños & Pereira-Menaut 1998:23.

94. Lariberus Breoroni
- 'Deo Lari/bero Br/eoron/i aram posu(it) […]VI …' (CIRG II, no.3).
- Location = Sanctuary of Donón, (Hio, Pontevedra).
- Dedicator = Unknown
- References = CIRG II, no.3; Baños & Pereira-Menaut 1998:23.

95. Lariberus (?)
- '[Deo L]/aribe/ro po/sui(t) a/ram pro [-c.1-] + [c.1.2-]/ […]' (CIRG II, no.5).
- Location = Sanctuary of Donón, (Hio, Pontevedra).
- Dedicator = Unknown
- References = CIRG II, no.5; Baños & Pereira-Menaut 1998:23.

96. Lariberus Breus
- '[Deo] / [Lari]/bero / Breo / aram / pos[uit] / […' (CIRG II, no.6).
- Location = Sanctuary of Donón, (Hio, Pontevedra).
- Dedicator = Unknown
- References = CIRG II, no.6; Baños & Pereira-Menaut 1998:24.

97. Lariberus Breus
- '[Deo La]/riber/o Bre/o ar[a-] / [m---] / …..' (CIRG II, no.7).
- Location = Sanctuary of Donón, (Hio, Pontevedra).
- Dedicator = Unknown
- References = CIRG II, 7; Baños & Pereira-Menaut 1998:24.

98. Lariberus Breus (?)
- '[Deo]/ [Lar]/[ibe]/r{r}o B/reo / ara- / [m …] /……' (CIRG II, no.9).

- Location = Sanctuary of Donón, (Hio, Pontevedra).
- Dedicator = Unknown
- References = CIRG II, no.9; Baños & Pereira-Menaut 1998:25; AE 1971, 192.

99. Lariberus Breus
- '[De]o Lar/ibe/ro B/[reo]/.....' (CIRG II, no.8).
- Location = Sanctuary of Donón, (Hio, Pontevedra).
- Dedicator = Unknown
- References = CIRG II, no.8; Baños & Pereira-Menaut 1998:25.

100. Lariberus
- 'Deo L/aribe/[ro...]/.....' (CIRG II, no.10).
- Location = Sanctuary of Donón, (Hio, Pontevedra).
- Dedicator = Unknown
- References = CIRG II, no.10; Baños & Pereira-Menaut 1998:25.

101. Lariberus
- 'Deo La/[ri]ber/[o...]/.....' (CIRG II, no.11).
- Location = Sanctuary of Donón, (Hio, Pontevedra).
- Dedicator = Unknown
- References = CIRG II, no.11; Baños & Pereira-Menaut 1998:26.

102. Lar-?
- 'Deo/ Lar./.....' (CIRG II, no.12).
- Location = Sanctuary of Donón, (Hio, Pontevedra).
- Dedicator = Unknown
- References = CIRG II, no.12; Baños & Pereira-Menaut 1998:26; AE 1971, 193.

103. Liberus Breus
- 'Deo L/iber/o Bre/o pos/u(it) ++++ / [...]' (CIRG II, no.4).
- Location = Sanctuary of Donón, (Hio, Pontevedra).
- Dedicator = Unknown
- References = Baños & Pereira-Menaut 1998:24; AE 1971, 191.

104. Lucoubus Arquienis
- 'Lucobu / Arquieni / Silonius / Silo / ex voto' (Arias Vilas, Le Roux & Tranoy 1979:no.68). Blázquez (1962:90) begins the inscription with 'Sacrum.'
- Location = Found in Sinoga (Rábada) (where it served to hold up a window).
- Dedicator = Silonius Silo
- References = Arias Vilas, Le Roux & Tranoy 1979:no.68; Tranoy 1981:289; IRG II 18; Blázquez 1962:90; ILER 868.

105. Lugubus Arquienobus
- 'Lugubo / Arquienob(o) / C(aius) Iulius / Hispanus / v(otum) s(oluit) l(ibens) m(erito)' (Arias Vilas, Le Roux & Tranoy 1979:no 67). ILER 869 has 'Lucubo / Arquieno' as the deity.
- Location = San Martín de Líñarán (Sober)
- Dedicator = C. Julius Hispanus
- References = Arias Vilas, Le Roux & Tranoy 1979:no.67; Tranoy 1981:289; IRG II 19; Blázquez 1962:90; ILER 869.

106. Navia
- 'Navia(e) / Ancetolu(s) Auri(ensis) exs C(inverted) (gens) / Sesm(acorum?) / votum possit / q(uoius) e(um) c(ompotum) f(ecit) (IRG I, 83).
- Location = Imprecise location in the Conventus Lucense
- Dedicator = Ancetolus, of the centuria Auriensis, the gens Sesmacorum?
- References = Tranoy 1981:294; CIL II 2601; IRG IV, 83; Blázquez 1962:180; ILER 892.

107. Navia
- 'Navi(a)e / l(ibens) ex v(oto) / a(ram) p(onendum) f(ecit) / p(ecunia) s(ua) c(urauit)' (IRG II, 7). The altar is decorated with squares and a crescent moon.
- Location = San Martín de Monte da Meda (Guntín, Lugo).
- Dedicator = Uncertain
- References = Arias Vilas, Le Roux & Tranoy 1979:no.71; IRG II 7; Blázquez 1962:179; Tranoy 1981:293-4; ILER 888.

108. Navia Arconunieca
- 'Naviae / Arcan/unieca(e) / [po]-su(it) / Max(imus) / ex vo/to' (IRG II, 6).
- Location = San Mamed de Lousada, near Santa Cristina de San Román, Guntín.
- Dedicator = Maximus
- References = IRG II, 6; Tranoy 1981:294; Arias Vilas, Le Roux & Tranoy 1979:no.72.

109. Navia Sesmaca
- 'Naviae / Sesma/cae v(otum) Anniu[s]' (IRG I, 82).
- Location = Imprecise location in the Conventus Lucense
- Dedicator = Unknown.
- References = Tranoy 1981:294; CIL II 2602; IRG IV, 82; Blázquez 1962:180; ILER 893.

110. Netaciveilebrica (?)
- 'Netaci/veilebricae : Sul/picius Se/verus / v(otum) s(oluit) l(ibens) m(erito)' (Arias Vilas, Le Roux & Tranoy 1979:no.18).
- Location = Imprecise location in the Conventus Lucense
- Dedicator = Sulpicius Severus (Roman name –Tranoy 1981:290).
- References = Arias Vilas, Le Roux & Tranoy 1979:no.18; Tranoy 1981:290; CIL II 2539; IRG II 69; Blázquez 1962:93; ILER 897.

111. Poemana
- 'Sacr/um Po/eman/ae collegium d/ivi aug' (CIL II 2573).
- Location = Lugo
- Dedicators = Collegium Divi Aug.
- References = CIL II 2573; Arias Vilas, Le Roux & Tranoy 1979:no.6.

112. Rea
- 'Reae / (hedera) Val(erius) / Opta/nus / v(otum) s(oluit) L(ibens) M(erito)' (Arias Vilas, Le Roux & Tranoy 1979:no.7).
- Location = Lugo
- Dedicator = Valerius Optanus
- References = Tranoy 1981:290; Arias Vilas, Le Roux & Tranoy 1979:no.7.

113. Rego
- 'Rego/ni M(?) S(?)' (Arias Vilas, Le Roux & Tranoy 1979:no.8). Blázquez considers this 'Regoni M(arti)'(1962:123) and Hübner proposes 'M(atris)' or 'M(agnae) S(acrum)' for the M.S. (CIL II, supp.1129). This M.S. may also be the first letters of the votive formula

(Tranoy 1981:290). ILER 912 has: 'Rego/ni v[o/tu]m s(oluit).'
- Location = Lugo
- Dedicator = Unknown.
- References = Tranoy 1981:290; Arias Vilas, Le Roux & Tranoy 1979:no.8; Blázquez 1962:123; CIL II 2574; IRG II 17; ILER 912; CIL II, supp.1129.

114. Reus Paramaecus
- 'Reo / Para/maeco / Aidi Po/thinus / et Prud(ens) / f(ilius) v(otum) s(olverunt) l(ibentes) m(erito)' (Arias Vilas, Le Roux & Tranoy 1979:no.9).
- Location = Lugo
- Dedicator = Pothinus and Prudens, sons of Aidius
- References = Tranoy 1981:290; Arias Vilas, Le Roux & Tranoy 1979:no.9.

115. Sannoava
- 'Sann/oava / C(aius) Fau/stus Fe/st(us) v(otum) s(oluit) l(ibens) m(erito)' (CIRG II, 106).
- Location = Campaño (Pontevedra)
- Dedicator = C. Faustus Festus (Roman tria-nomina).
- References = CIRG II, no.106; Blázquez 2001:178; Tranoy 1981:291.

116. Soe Meobrigus
- 'Soe Me/obrigo / f(ecit) Parvi/[llius]/-----' (CIRG I, no.86). To 'So Meobrigo' (Tranoy 1981:290).
- Loc = Imprecise location in the Conventus Lucense
- Dedicator = Parvillius?
- References = Tranoy 1981:290; CIRG I, no.86; Blázquez 2001:176; IRG I, 23.

117. Veroca
- 'Veroce / Pa(ternus) Primi (filius) / ex vo/to' (Arias Vilas, Le Roux & Tranoy 1979:no.11). As 'Vero' in CIL II 2577, 'Vero[r]e' in IRG II 14, Blázquez 1962:217 and ILER 952.
- Location = Lugo
- Dedicator = Paternus, son of Primus
- References = Arias Vilas, Le Roux & Tranoy 1979:no.11; Tranoy 1981:294; CIL II 2577; IRG II 14; Blázquez 1962:217; ILER 952.

118. Verora
- 'Verore / Rufus / Me (?) ex / visu' (Arias Vilas, Le Roux & Tranoy 1979:no.12).
- Location = Lugo
- Dedicator = Rufus
- References = Arias Vilas, Le Roux & Tranoy 1979:no.12; Tranoy 1981:294; CIL II 2576; IRG II 13; Blázquez 1962:217; ILER 953.

119. Ver(ore)
- 'Ver(ore) / [.] cer/...' (Arias Vilas, Le Roux & Tranoy 1979:no.13).
- Location = Lugo
- Dedicator = Unknown
- References = Arias Vilas, Le Roux & Tranoy 1979:no.13; Tranoy 1981:294; CIL II 2578; IRG II 16; ILER 955.

120. Vestius Aloniecus
- 'Deo V/estio / Aloni/eco ar/am p(osuit) Sev/era / -------' (CIRG II, no.107).
- Location = Lourizán, a site on the south side of the ría of Pontevedra.
- Dedicator = Severa
- References = CIRG II, no.107; Blázquez 2001:178 & 1962:99-102; Tranoy 1981:290-1; IRG III, 27; ILER 949.

121. Vestius Aloniecus
- 'Deo / Vesti/[o A]loni/[e]co ar/[am p(osuit)]/------' (CIRG II, 108).
- Location = Lourizán, a site on the south side of the ría of Pontevedra.
- Dedicator = Uncertain
- References = Tranoy 1981:290-1; IRG III, 28; Blázquez 1962:99-102; ILER 950.

122. Virrora Villaegus
- 'Virrore / Viliaego / Aitanius / Paternus / v(otum) s(oluit) l(ibens) m(erito)' (Arias Vilas, Le Roux & Tranoy 1979:no.14). Dedicator as: 'Altmiius' (CIL II 2575), 'Attanius' (IRG II, 15 & Blázquez 1962:218), and 'Attarius' (ILER 951). IRG II, 15 has 'Viliaeco' for the deity surname.
- Location = Lugo
- Dedicator = Aitanius Paternus
- References = Arias Vilas, Le Roux & Tranoy 1979:no.14; Tranoy 1981:294; CIL II 2575; IRG II, 15; Blázquez 1962:218; ILER, 951.

Uncertain Reading from the Conventus Lucense

123. ....ae (Navia?)
- '........ae / [sacru]m / C(aius) Valerius / Carus / miles l(egionis) X (Decimae) G(eminae) / v(otum) s(olvit) l(ibens) m(erito)' (Arias Vilas, Le Roux & Tranoy 1979:no.75). Due to the termination of the deity name in 'a' and the proximity of this dedication to the river Navia, Arais Vilas, Le Roux and Tranoy (1979:no.75) and Tranoy (1981:294) take this to be a dedication to Navia.
- Location = S. Román de Cervantes (Lugo).
- Dedicator = Caius Valerius Carus, a soldier of the Legio X Gemina.
- References = Arias Vilas, Le Roux & Tranoy 1979:no.75; Tranoy 1981:294; García y Bellido 1966:28; ILER 1014.

124. --erbo Erbieco
- '[-c.5-]/erbo / Erbie/co L(---) S(---) E(---)/ ex vot/o p(osuit) l(ibens) a(nimo)' (CIRG I, no.20).
- Location = In the church of San Pedro de Herbogo (Rois).
- Dedicator = Unknown
- References = Blázquez 2001:176; CIRG I, no.20.

125. ...Remigus?
- '.../...migo / Cornelia / [R]ufina / ex visu / libens / merito' (Arias Vilas, Le Roux & Tranoy 1979:no.15). It only retains part of the deity's surname.
- Location = Lugo
- Dedicator = Cornelia Rufina
- References = Tranoy 1981:291; Arias Vilas, Le Roux & Tranoy 1979:no.15; IRG II, 25.

Conventus Asturum

126. Aegiamunniaegus
- 'Aegiamun/niaego / Anistius / Placidus / Cili filius / Alterniacinus / v(otum) s(oluit) l(ibens) m(erito)' (IRG IV, 90).
- Location = Viana del Bollo (Orense)

- Dedicator = Antistius Placidus, son of Clivus, from the clan Alterniaicinus
- References = IRG IV 90; Tranoy 1981:296; CIL II 2523; Blázquez 1962:71; ILER, 706.

127. Aernus
- 'Deo / [A]erno / Lucr(etius) / Valens / ex / voto' (Blázquez 1962:66).
- Location = Malta (Macedo de Cavaleiros)
- Dedicator = Lucretius Valens
- References = Blázquez 1962:66; Tranoy 1981:296; IRG III, 29; Encarnação 1975:83; ILER, 710.

128. Aernus
- 'Deo / Aerno / Ordo / Zoelara / ex voto' (CIL II 2606).
- Location = Castro de Avelâs, near Bragance.
- Dedicator = The 'Ordo Zoelarum'
- References = Tranoy 1981:296; CIL II 2606; Blázquez 1962:65; Leite de Vasconcelos 1905:338; Encarnação 1975:79-80; ILER, 709.

129. Aernus
- 'Deo Aer/no M./[Pl]acidi/[u]s [P]laci/[d]ianus / v(otum) l(ibens) r(eddiddit) or r(etulit)' (AE 1992, 995). Also: 'Deo Aer/no M/acidi' (CIL II 5651; Encarnação 1975:82) and as: 'Veror[e] / mu(lier) e(x) v(oto) / h(anc) a(ram) s(oluit)' (IRG III, 29). ILER 712 has: 'deo A(e)rno M. Acidi.' 'Aernus' in Tranoy (1981:296) and Blázquez (1962:65).
- Location = Castro de Avelâs, near Bragance.
- Dedicator= Unsure
- References = AE 1992, 995; Blázquez 1962:65; Tranoy 1981:296; CIL II 5651; IRG III, 29; Encarnação 1975:82; ILER 712.

130. Bodus
- 'Deo Bo/do Vei/cius vo/tu(m) / s(oluit) l(ibens) m(erito)' (Quintana Prieto 1969:43).
- Location = Villadepalos (Carracedelo, León).
- Dedicator = Veicius
- References = Quintana Prieto 1969:43-5; Tranoy 1981:297; CIL II 5670; Blázquez 1962:208 & 1970:72; ILER 767.

131. Caraedudius
- 'Caraedudi / Fronto Re/burri f(ilius) / v(otum) s(oluit) l(ibens) m(erito)' (Mañanez Perez 1982:no.101).
- Location = Astorga
- Dedicator = Fronto, son of Reburrus
- References = Tranoy 1981:297; Mañanez Perez 1982:no.101; CIL II 5663; Blázquez 1962:76; ILER 777.

132. Cosus
- 'Cos[sue?] / S( ) ? Fla[vi]/us Tu[ro]/ni (filius) ex [v]/oto l(ibens) [s(oluit)]' (AE 1983, 592).
- Location = S. Estebán del Toral, Bembibre
- Dedicator = S. Flavius son of Turonus
- References = AE 1983, 592.

133. Cosus
- 'Cos[sue] / Log[ius?] Pac[…/ v(otum) s(oluit) l(ibens) m(erito)]' (AE 1983, 595).
- Location = El Valle
- Dedicator = Log… Pac…
- References = AE 1983, 595.

134. Cosus
- 'Dei (sic) Co(ssue) / Calu(i)/celae(o) / B or Delaesu/ Sonelaio ex [vo(to)?] +' (AE 1999, 914).
- Location = Villasumil, Candín, León.
- Dedicator = Caluicelaeus Delaesus (or Belaesus) Sonelaius?
- References = AE 1999, 914; AE 1998, 760.

135. Cosiovi Ascannus
- 'Cosi/ovi Asca/nno / sacrum' (Mañanez Perez 1982:no.103). In Tranoy has 'Cosius Viascannus' (1981:297).
- Location = Laciana (Las Rozas, Villablino, León, region of Bierzo).
- Dedicator = Unknown.
- References = Mañanez Perez 1982:no.103; Tranoy 1981:297; Blázquez 1962:118; ERA, 232.

136. Cossua Nedoledius
- 'Cossue N/edoledi / Flavinus / Flavi a(ram) p(osuit)' (HE 1989, no.397). In Mañanez Perez (1982:no.104), line 1-2 = 'Cossue n/idoledio,' and line 4 = 'Flavi a(nimo) p(osuit).' In AE 1967, 233: 'Cossue N/idoiedio / Ipauinus / Klasa a(ram) p(osuit).'
- Location = Noceda del Bierzo (Bierzo).
- Dedicator = Flavinus, son of Flavus
- References = HE 1989, no.397; Tranoy 1981:297; Mañanez Perez 1982:no.104; AE 1967, 233.

137. Cossua Segidiaecus
- 'Deo Domino / Cossue / Segidi/aeco. L(ucius) Aur(elius) Fr(onto) / ex voto / l(ibens) m(erito) p(osuit)' (Mañanez Perez 1982:no.105).
- Location = Arlanza (Bierzo)
- Dedicator = L. Aurelius Fronto
- References = Mañanez Perez 1982:no.105; AE, 1967, 232; Tranoy 1981:297.

138. Cosus Tueranaeus(?) Parameius(?)
- 'C[o]s[sue] / Tue[ran]/ae(o) Pa[ra]meio / T(itus) Fla[us / m(iles)]? l(egionis) VII G(eminae) […] / v(otum) p(osuit) a(nimo) [l(ibens)]' (AE 1983, 593).
- Location = El Valle
- Dedicator = Titus Flaus, soldier of the Legio VII Gemina
- Reference = AE 1983, 593.

139. Cosus Udunaeus Itilienue?
- 'Co[ssue] / V[d]una[eo] / Itilien[u]e / M(arcus) Iuliu[s / Pa]ter[n]us le[g( )?] u[…] / ex v[oto …]' (AE 1983, 594).
- Location = El Valle
- Dedicator = Marcus Iulius Paternus?
- References = AE 1983, 594.

140. Crarus
- 'Augo Prop/eddi Craro / votum / s(oluit) l(ibens) m(erito)' (Mañanez Perez 1982:no.106).
- Location = San Miguel de Laciana (Villablino)
- Dedicator = Augo, son of Propeddus
- References = Tranoy 1981:297; Mañanez Perez 1982:no.106; Quintana Prieto 1969:.49-51; ILER, 747.

141. Dea Canduedia
- 'Deae / Candu/ediae / sacru/m cas/tellani' (AE 1995, 855).
- Location = S. Esteban del Toral, Bembibre (terr. of Interamnium Flavium), León.
- Dedicator = Unsure

- References = AE 1995, 855; Mangas & Olano 1995:339.

142. Dea Deganta
    - 'Deae / Deganti(ae) / Flavia Fl(avii) / in hono(rem) / Argel(orum) / f(ecit) v(otum)' (Quintana Prieto 1969:57).
    - Location = Cacabelos (Bierzo).
    - Dedicator = Flavia, daughter of Flavus, in honorem Argel(orum?)
    - References = Quintana Prieto 1969:57-9; Tranoy 1981:298; CIL II 5672; Blázquez 1962:77; ILER, 799.

143. Densus
    - 'Denso / Var(u)s C(aii) f(ilius) / libens dicauit' (Encarnação 1975:174).
    - Location = Cilhades (Felgar, Moncorvo).
    - Dedicator = Unknown.
    - References = Tranoy 1981:298; Encarnação 1975:173-4.

144. Deus Equernurus
    - 'Deis E/quernur(is)? / Iulius / Reburrus / v(otum) s(oluit) l(ibens) m(erito)' (HE 1989, no.412).
    - Location = La Pola de Gordón, León.
    - Dedicator = Julius Reburrus
    - References = HE 1989, no.412.

145. (Evedutonius) Barciaecus
    - 'L(ucius) Ser(vius) Secun(dus) / Evedutoniu / Barciaeco / v(otum) s(oluit) l(ibens) m(erito)'(ERA no.10). The 'Evedutonius' which proceeds this is thought by F. Diego Santos (ERA no.10) to be part of the deity name, but Tranoy (1981:296-7), Blázquez (1962:75) and Albertos Firmat (1975:54-55) all agree that Barciaecus is the sole deity name, and take the 'Evedutoniu(m)' to be a gens name, following the dedicators name.
    - Location = Naraval (Tineo), Oviedo
    - Dedicator = L. Servius Secundus
    - References = ERA, no.10; Tranoy 1981:296-7; Blázquez 1962:75; ILER, 765.

146. Mandica
    - 'L(ucius) Pompeius Pa/ternu(s) / Mandic/ae v. m./ s.' (ILER 876). As 'Mamdicae' in CIL II 5669.
    - Location = Ponferrada
    - Dedicator = L. Pompeius Paternus
    - References = Quintana Prieto 1969:66; Tranoy 1981:298; CIL II 5669; Blázquez 1962:61-2; ILER 876.

147. Mentoviacus
    - 'Mentoviaco / Caris… …Of/ono ex voto' (Blázquez 1962:107).
    - Location = Villalcampo
    - Dedicator = Unknown
    - References = Tranoy 1981:298; Blázquez 1962:107-8; ILER 879.

148. Nidanlua
    - 'Nida/nlua / [---]' (AE 1990, 550). A votive altar decorated with a bulls head and a crescent moon.
    - Location = S. Estaban del Toral, Ponferrada.
    - Dedicator = Unsure
    - References = AE 1990, 550.

149. Nimmedus Seddiagus
    - 'Nimmedo / Seddiago / G(aius) Sulpicius / Africanus / v(otum) s(oluit) l(ibens) m(erito)' (ERA no.9).
    - Location = Ujo (Mieres, Oviedo)
    - Dedicator = G. Sulpicius Africanus
    - References = Tranoy 1981:298; ERA, 9; Blázquez 1962:213-4; ILER 900.

150. Tillenus
    - 'Q Iul / Tiro / Tilleno / v. s. l. m.' (Albertos Firmat 1974:151).
    - Location = S. Martiño de Viloria (Barco de Valdeorras, Orense)
    - Dedicator = Q. Iulius Tiro
    - References = Albertos Firmat 1974:151; Tranoy 1981:299.

151. Udunnaecus
    - 'Vdunn/aeco C(aius) Iuniu/s Silanus / v(otum) s(oluit) l(ibens) m(erito)' (AE 1983, 591). The last '-co' of the deity name may be interpreted as 'Cosus' perhaps (AE 1983, 591).
    - Location = Santibañez, Bembibre
    - Dedicator = Caius Iunius Silanus
    - References = AE 1983, 591.

152. Vacocaburius
    - 'de(o) Vac/ocabu/rio' (ILER 946).
    - Location = Astorga
    - Dedicator = Unknown.
    - References = Mañanez Perez 1982:no.1; Tranoy 1981:299; CIL II 5666; Blázquez 1962:113; Quintana Prieto 1969:78-80; ILER 946.

153. Vacodonnaegus
    - 'Deo Vacodonnaego / sacrum Resp(ublica) / Ast(uricae) Aug(ustae) per / mag(istratus) G(aium) Pacatum / et Fl(avium) Proculum / ex donis / curante Iulio Nepote' (Mañanez Perez 1982:no.108). Inscribed on a plaque.
    - Location = La Milla del Río (20km east of Astorga).
    - Dedicator = 'Res Publica Asturica Augusta,' Representatives = 2 magistrates, G. Pacatus and Flavius Proculus (Roman names), person responsible for the organization: Iulius Nepos.
    - References = Mañanez Perez 1982:no.108; Tranoy 1981:299; CIL II 2636; Blázquez 1962:164; Quintana Prieto 1969:81-84; ILER 947.

Uncertain Reading from the Conventus Asturum

154. Asturice (deity?)
    - 'Asturice / [sacr]um Cae/[si]nius Ag[ri]cola eq(ues) / [1-2] Fl(aviae) I Lusit(anorum) / [C]urator' (HE 1989, no.384).
    - Location = Found in Astorga in 1986.
    - Dedicator = Caesinius (or Caesianius) Agricola, of Flaviae I Lusitanorum.
    - References = HE 1989, no.384; AE 1987, 611.

155. …ovius Tabaliaenus
    - '…ovi/o Taba/liaeno / Luggo/ni Argan/ticaeni / haec mon(umenta) / possierunt' (ERA, no.11). Blázquez (1962:95) has: '(I)ovi/o Taba/liaeno.' ILER 806 has: '[Du]lovi/o Taba/lieno' as the deity. The altar is mutilated and the deity name is incomplete, and the many attempts to resolve this all remain inconclusive (Tranoy 1981:299).
    - Location = Grases (Villaviciosa, Oviedo)
    - Dedicator = The Luggoni Arganticaeni
    - References = Tranoy 1981:299; ERA 11; Blázquez 1962:95; ILER 807.

Catalogue II
Classical Deities in the North-West of Hispania

Conventus Bracaraugustanus

1. Asclepius and Hygia
   - 'Asclepio / et Hygiae / Marcus / ex voto' (CIL II 2411).
   - Location = Braga
   - Dedicator = Marcus
   - References = Tranoy 1981:310; CIL II 2411; ILER 183.

2. Concordia (of the citizens of the Municipality)
   - '[Con]cordia[e] / munici[p]u[m] / municipi / Aquiflaviens(is) / L(ucius) Valerius / Longinus / de suo' (AE 1973, 304).
   - Location = Aquae Flaviae (Chaves).
   - Dedicator = L. Valerius Longinus
   - References = Tranoy 1981:311; Ramirez 1981:245; AE 1973, 304.

3. Cybele
   - 'Matri deum / Gelasius / Caesaria' (ILER 373).
   - Location = Chaves
   - Dedicator = Gelasis and Caesaria(nus?)
   - References = ILER 373; Tranoy 1981:334; Rodríguez Colmenero 1977:334.

4. Cybele
   - 'Ma(tri) De/um Alb/uia Pa/terna vo. so(luit)' (ILER 378).
   - Location = Marco de Canaveses
   - Dedicator = Albuia Paterna
   - References = ILER 378; Tranoy 1981:334.

5. Deus
   - 'Allius Reburri rogo deu(m) adiutorem in ac conducta conservada qi(s)qis in ac conducta p(ossessionem) mici aut meis involaverit si r(emps) quaecunque res et mii it a(…) v(…) s(…) si(…) l(…) siquit ea res v(…) s(…) l(…) v(…) f(…) Danceroi' (Alarcão 1988, Vol.II:1/56).
   - Location = Rameseiros, Vilar de Perdizes, Montalegre.
   - Dedicator = Allius son of Reburrus.
   - References = Alarcão 1988, Vol.II:1/56; CIL II 2476.

6. Diana
   - 'Capito / Siiviir/(us) ara(m) pon/o sanct/(e) Diianii' (Rodríguez Colmenero 1977:335).
   - Location = La Mezquita (Orense)
   - Dedicator = Capito Siiviirus
   - References = Rodríguez Colmenero 1977:335; Tranoy 1981:313.

7. Diana
   - 'Deane / Fa(bius) Sat/urni/nus / ex v(oto) p(osuit)' (IRG IV, 71).
   - Location = Monte Louredo (Between the cities of Reza and Freijiendo, Orense).
   - Dedicator = Fabius Saturninus
   - References = Tranoy 1981:313; Ramirez 1981:244; IRG IV, 71; ILER 5958; EE, IX, 280.

8. Diana
   - 'Dianae / sac(rum) / Q. Valerius? / Victor / ex mo/nitu /era' (AE 1994, 937).
   - Location = Bande, Orense.
   - Dedicator = Q. Valerius? Victor
   - References = AE 1994, 937.

9. Di
   - 'Diis cum hoc/ et lacum quo / voto misce/tur / G.C(- - -) Calp(urnius) Rufi/nus u(ir) c(larissimus)' (AE 1997, 861). Though Rodríguez Colmenero has 'Diis cua aede/ et la(cu).cum.cavi[s]/ voto misce[n]/tur H[ostiae] / G(neus) C(aius) Calp(urnius) Rufi/nus e(x) voto' (1993:68).
   - Location = Santuary of Panóias, (Assentos, Vale de Nogueira, Vila Real).
   - Dedicator = G.C. Calpurnius Rufinus
   - References = AE 1997, 861; CIL II 2395d; Rodríguez Colmenero 1993:67-9; Tranoy 1981:337; Alarcão 1988:Vol.II,1/386.

10. Di
    - 'Diis [deabusque temple] / huius Hostiae quae ca/dunt hic immolantur / Exta intra quadrata / contra cremantur / Sanguis laciculis iuxta / superfunditur / [G. C(- - -) Calp(urnius) Rufinus u(ir) c(larissimus)]' (AE 1997, 857). In CIL II 2395e: 'Huius hostiae quae ca/dunt hic immolantur/exta intra quadrata/ contra cremantur / sanctus lac . KVII spacto /superfu...tur.' Rodríguez Colmenero has: 'Diis [loci] huius hostiae quae cadunt …etc.' (1993:63).
    - Location = Santuary of Panóias, (Assentos, Vale de Nogueira, Vila Real).
    - Dedicator = Unsure
    - References = AE 1997, 857; CIL II 2395e; Rodríguez Colmenero 1993:62-3; Tranoy 1981:337; Alarcão 1988:Vol.II,1/386.

11. Di, Deae, All Numina, and the Numina Lapitearum
    - 'Diis Deabusque ae/ternum lacum omni/busque numinibus/ et Lapitearum.cum hoc templo sacrauit / G.C. Calp(urnius) Rufinus u(ir) c(larissimus) / in quo.hostiae voto/cremantur' (Rodríguez Colmenero 1993:63).
    - Location = Santuary of Panóias, (Assentos, Vale de Nogueira, Vila Real).
    - Dedicator = G.C. Calpurnius Rufinus
    - References = AE 1997, 859; CIL II 2395b; Rodríguez Colmenero 1993:63-5; Tranoy 1981:336; Alarcão 1988:Vol.II,1/386.

12. Di Severis
    - 'Diis Seve[r]is in hoc / templo lo[ca]t[i]s / aedem G [C(- - -) C]alp(urnius) Ru/finus u(ir) [c(larissimus)]' (AE 1997, 858). Though Rodríguez Colmenero proposes the following interpretation: 'Diis Sev(eris) Man(ibus) Diis ira/tis [ded(icauit)] lacum et/aedem [C(neus)] C(aius) Calp(urnius) Ru/finus' (1993:70).
    - Location = Santuary of Panóias, (Assentos, Vale de Nogueiras, Vila Real).
    - Dedicator = G.C. Calpurnius Rufinus
    - References = AE 1997, 858; CIL II 2395a; Rodríguez Colmenero 1993:69-70; Tranoy 1981:337; Alarcão 1988:Vol.II,1/386.

13. Eventus
    - 'Deo Sa/ncto Ev/ento Fl/ Fronto / ex praec/epto' (CIL II 2412).
    - Location = Braga
    - Dedicator = Flavus Fronto
    - References = Tranoy 1981:311; Ramirez 1981:245; CIL II 2412; ILER, 433.

14. Fortuna
- 'D(eae) S(anctae) / For/tunae / Val(erius) Pa/ternus / ex v(oto) p(osuit)' (AE 1997, 854).
- Location = Freixo (Tongobriga), Marco de Canaveses.
- Dedicator = Valerius Paternus
- References = AE 1997, 854.

15. Genius
- 'Genio / Satur/ninus / Catur/onis f/ v s l a' (CIL II 6338f).
- Location = Alvarelhos (Santo Tirso)
- Dedicator = Saturninus, son of Caturo
- References = Tranoy 1981:322; CIL II 6338 f; ILER 543.

16. Genius
- 'Q(uintus) Sabi/nius Flo/rus Gen/io v(otum) s(oluit) l(ibens) m(erito)' (AE 1987, 563).
- Location = Caires, Amares, Braga.
- Dedicator = Quintus Sabinius Florus
- References = AE 1987, 563.

17. Genius Populi Romani
- '.......P(opuli?) R(omani?) / C(aius) Marc(ius) Maxi(mus) / (centurion?) leg(ionis) / VIII G(eminae) p(iae) f(elicis) / v(otum) s(oluit) l(ibens) m(erito)' (IRG IV, 100).
- Location = S. Tome (Orense)
- Dedicator = Gaius Marcus Maximus(?).
- References = CIL II 2522; IRG IV,100; ILER 545; Tranoy 1981:322.

18. Hercules
- 'Hercule' (the only word inscribed on this altar : Alarcâo 1988, Vol.II:1/50).
- Location = S. Mamede de Lindoso, Ponte de Bracara.
- Dedicator = Unknown
- References = Alarcâo 1988, Vol.II:1/50; AE 1983:587.

19. Isis
- 'Insidi / Cornelia / Saturnina / ex voto' (Rodríguez Colmenero 1977:337).
- Location = Samaiôes, Chaves
- Dedicator = Cornelia Saturnina
- References = Tranoy 1981:334; Rodríguez Colmenero 1977:337.

20. Isis Augusta
- 'Isidi Aug sacrum / Lucretia Fida sacred . perp / Rom et Aug / Conventuus Bracaraug d' (CIL II 2416).
- Location = Braga
- Dedicator = Lucretia Fida, a priestess of the Conventus
- References = CIL II 2416; Tranoy 1981:334; ILER 352.

21. Juno
- 'Iuno Meiruranarum / Quintillo et Prisco cos' (CIL II 2409).
- Location = Monte Cristelo (Guimarâes)
- Dedicator = Uncertain
- References = Tranoy 1981:311; CIL II 2409; Tovar 1964-5:247-8, no.5.

22. Juno
- 'Iunoni / ...ris / Deum / [A]emilia / Flavina' (IRG IV, 70).
- Location = Albarelos (Monterrey, Verín).
- Dedicator = Emilia Flavina
- References = IRG IV, 70; Tranoy 1981:311; Ramirez 1981:245; CIL II 2521; Rodríguez Colmenero 1977:334.

23. Jupiter
- 'Fl(avius) Flav/i Iovi / votum s(oluit) / l(ibens) a(nimo)' (IRG IV, 65).
- Location = Guïn (Bande).
- Dedicators = Flavus, son of Flavus.
- References = Tranoy 1981:317; Ramirez 1981:242; IRG IV, 65; ILER 63.

24. Jupiter
- 'Iovi' (CIL II 5568 – fragmentary inscription).
- Location = Negrelos
- Dedicators = Unknown
- References = Tranoy 1981:318; CIL II 5568.

25. Jupiter
- 'Iovi' (AE 1981,533).
- Location = S. Salvador de Arnoia, Orense.
- Dedicator = Unsure
- References = AE 1981, 533; Tranoy 1981:318.

26. Jupiter
- 'Iovi.../ Oletv... / lind...' (EE VIII, 114). Difficult to read as it is a fragment.
- Location = Braga
- Dedicators = Unknown
- References = Tranoy 1981:317; EE VIII, 114.

27. Jupiter
- 'Iov/ fil / se' (EE IX, 262).
- Location = Castelo de Aguiar (Villa Pouca d'Aguiar).
- Dedicators = Unknown
- References = Tranoy 1981:318; EE IX, 262.

28. Jupiter
- On the first side: 'Med/amu/[s...],' and on the right side: 'Iov/ l. v. s.' (in which the l.u.s may be l(ibens) v(otum) s(oluit)) (AE 1973, 321).
- Location = Monte Mozinho, Penafiel
- Dedicator = Medamus
- References = AE 1973, 321; Tranoy 1981:317.

29. Jupiter Depulsor
- 'Iovi / (D)epulsori / (Du)rmia / (P)usinna / (e)x voto / (p)osuit' (CIL II 2414).
- Location = S. Martín de Dume (next to Braga)
- Dedicators = Durmia Pusinna
- References = Tranoy 1981:316; Ramirez 1981:243; CIL II 2414; ILER 102.

30. Jupiter Maximus
- 'Iovi M/aximo / Vicani / Atucause / ....' (CIL II 6287).
- Location = Amarante
- Dedicators = The 'Vicani Atucauseses'
- References = Tranoy 1981:316; CIL II 6287; ILER 85.

*See Nabia Corona (No.49, Cat.I) for another Jupiter dedication.

31. Jupiter Optimus Maximus
- 'Iovi O (M) / pro salute / triari ma(gni?) / leg iur c v / et proculae/ eius Aemil Cr(es)/cens comes v s l m' (CIL II 2415) (may be 'Leg(atus) iur(idicum) c(larissimum) v(irum)').
- Location = Braga
- Dedicators = Aemilius Crescens

- References = Tranoy 1981:316; CIL II, 2415; ILER 19.

32. Jupiter Optimus Maximus
- 'I O M / vot sol/ mil leg / VII Gem / Catullino et Apro / cos' (CIL II 2389). ILER 55 has: 'Pullin[us P.]' in the place of 'Catullino et Apro cos.'
- Location = Trêsminas
- Dedicator = Soldier of Legio VII Geminae
- References = CIL II 2389; ILER 55; Tranoy 1981:316.

33. Jupiter Optimus Maximus
- 'I.O.M. / mil . ch/ I Galli/cae . eq. / c.r.v.s / l.m' (EE, VIII, 109).
- Location = Ribeirinha
- Dedicators = Mil. Coh. I Gall.
- References = EE, VIII, 109; ILER 86; Tranoy 1981:316.

34. Jupiter Optimus Maximus
- 'Iovi O/ptimo / Maximo / Sulpici/us Sulpi/cianus qu/ot vouit' (AE 1979, 362).
- Location = Caldas de Vizela
- Dedicators = Sulpicius Sulpicianus
- References = AE 1979, 362; Tranoy 1981:316.

35. Jupiter Optimus Maximus
- 'I(ovi) O(ptimo) M(aximo) / Ligarius / Sabinus / v(otum) s(oluit) l(ibens) m(erito)' (AE 1981, 531).
- Location = (S. Munio de) Veiga, A Bola (Celanova)
- Dedicators = Ligarius Sabinus
- References = AE 1981, 531; Tranoy 1981:316.

36. Jupiter Optimus Maximus
- 'L(ucius) Cas(sius) Caen(icus) / Tamac(anus) (centuria) Nem(…?) / dec(urio) al(ae) (primae) Gig(urrorum) / comp(luribus) bel(lis) torque(ibus) / [p]hale(ris) [bi Nem(…?) / dec(urio) al(ae) (primae) Gig(urrorum) / comp(luribus) bel(lis) torque(ibus) / [p]hale(ris) [bi]s donatus / Iovi O(ptimo) M(aximo) v(otum) s(oluit) / l(ibens) a(nimo)' (AE 1976, 296).
- Location = Castrelo del Valle
- Dedicators = L. Cassius Caenicus
- References = AE 1976, 296; Tranoy 1981:316.

37. Jupiter Optimus Maximus
- 'Iovi O(ptimo) Max(imo) Capito Cap(itionis) v(otum) l(ibens) a(nimo) s(oluit)' (Rodríguez Colmenero & Lourenço Fontes 1980:30-1).
- Location = Vilar de Perdizes
- Dedicators = Capito Cap.
- References = Rodríguez Colmenero & Lourenço Fontes 1980:30-1; AE 1980, 578; Tranoy 1981:316.

38. • Jupiter Optimus Maximus
- Jupiter Optimus Maximus (Tranoy 1981:317).
- Location = Carvalho de Rei
- Dedicator = Publius Flavius, son of Cileiovus
- References = Tranoy 1981:317.

39. Jupiter Optimus Maximus
- 'I.O.M./ Vc Vti/pnus / ex vo/to' (CIL II 2388).
- Location = Ribeira
- Dedicator = Uc(…?) Utipnus
- References = CIL II 2388; Tranoy 1981:317.

40. Jupiter Optimus Maximus
- 'I.O.M./ l. p. / Reb / Reburrus/ l. p.' (Leite de Vasconcelos 1913:223,229).
- Location = Mateus, Vila Real
- Dedicator = Reb. Reburrus
- References = Leite de Vasconcelos 1913:223,229; Tranoy 1981:317.

41. Jupiter Optimus Maximus
- 'I.O.M. / ex voto / Flociflorebi / Florebus Fortunatus / posuit' (CIL II 2608).
- Location = Vilarelho da Raia.
- Dedicators = Florebus Fortunatus, (son of Flociflorebus?)
- References = CIL II 2608; ILER 145; Tranoy 1981:317.

42. Jupiter Optimus Maximus
- 'Iovi Op/timo M/aximo / ap Sa/binus / Prob/i . f'(CIL II 2495).
- Location = Friâes
- Dedicators = Sabinus, son of Probus
- References = CIL II 2445; ILER 88; Tranoy 1981:317.

43. Jupiter Optimus Maximus
- '…/ Rufi Gro/vius votu/m Iovi Opt/tumo M/axumo / …' (ILER 58).
- Location = Vila Mou.
- Dedicators = Grovius, son of Rufus
- References = ILER 58, Tranoy 1981:317; EE IX, 268.

44. Jupiter Optimus Maximus
- 'Matern/us posuit / arundam / Iovi Opti/mo Max/imo' (AE 1982, 566).
- Location = Châo Grande, S. Maria de Bouro, Braga.
- Dedicators = Maternus
- References = AE 1982, 566; AE 1983, 554; Tranoy 1981:317; 34.

45. Jupiter Optimus Maximus
- 'Iovi / Nispro / ex voto' (CIL II 5567).
- Location = Mosteiro
- Dedicators = Nispro
- References = Tranoy 1981:317; CIL II 5567; ILER 143.

46. Jupiter Optimus Maximus
- 'Iovi Opt/mo Mx/u c a o r' (EE IX, 274).
- Location = Tronco, near the Concelho de Monforte de Rio Leivre (Chaves)
- Dedicators = V. Car? (Tranoy 1981:317).
- References = EE IX, 274; Tranoy 1981:317.

47. Jupiter Optimus Maximus
- 'Iovi / op. m. / P L P / V N M' (ILER 5941).
- Location = Sanfins
- Dedicators = Unsure
- References = ILER 5941; Tranoy 1981:317.

48. • Jupiter Optimus Maximus
- Jupiter Optimus Maximus (Tranoy 1981:317)
- Location = S. Comba (Bande)
- Dedicators = Unknown
- References = Tranoy 1981:317; Unpublished.

49. Jupiter Optimus Maximus
- 'I(ovi) O(ptimo) M(aximo) / Cor(nelius?) /…/V(otum)…' (IRG IV, 114). Rodríguez Colmenero has 'Cor(ia)..' rather than 'Cor(nelius?)' (1977:333).
- Location = Orense (Palacio Episcopal).
- Dedicators = Cornelius?

- References = Tranoy 1981:317; IRG IV, 114; ILER 66; Rodríguez Colmenero 1977:333.

50. • Jupiter Optimus Maximus
- Jupiter Optimus Maximus (Tranoy 1981:317)
- Location = Noalla
- Dedicators = Unknown
- References = Tranoy 1981:317; Unpublished.

51. Jupiter Optimus Maximus
- 'I(ovi) O(ptimo) M(aximo) / Certi(us) / ...rus/ ...uci / v(otum) l(ibens) a(nimo) s(oluit)' (Rodríguez Colmenero 1977:332).
- Location = Seoane de Oleiros
- Dedicators = Certius...?
- References = Rodríguez Colmenero 1977:332; Tranoy 1981:317.

52. Jupiter Optimus Maximus
- 'I(ovi) O(ptimo) M(aximo) / ou[ante]r? / v(otum) s(oluit) T(itus) R(ufus?)' (AE 1974, 395).
- Location = Layoso
- Dedicators = T(itus) R(ufus?)
- References = AE 1974, 395; Tranoy 1981:317.

53. Jupiter Optimus Maximus
- 'Iovi / Optumo / Max(umo) ex / voto / posuit S. Si[...]' (AE 1971, 194).
- Location = Tintores, Verín
- Dedicators = Unknown
- References = Tranoy 1981:317; AE 1971, 194.

54. Jupiter Optimus Maximus
- '[I]ovi / O(ptimo) M(aximo) / [R]ufo...' (IRG IV, 68).
- Location = Nocelo da Pena, Ginzo de Limia
- Dedicators = Rufo...?
- References = IRG IV, 68; Tranoy 1981:317; ILER 67.

55. Jupiter Optimus Maximus
- 'Iovi Op(timo) / Maximo / L... ...S / v(otum) s(oluit) l(ibens) m(erito)' (IRG IV, 67).
- Location = Ganade, Ginzo de Limia.
- Dedicators = Unknown
- References = IRG IV, 67; Tranoy 1981:317.

56. • Jupiter Optimus Maximus
- Jupiter Optimus Maximus (Tranoy 1981:317)
- Location = Villaverde da Raia.
- Dedicators = Unknown
- References = Tranoy 1981:317; Unpublished.

57. Jupiter Optimus Maximus
- 'Iovi / O M / v o m / a s' (EE IX, 271).
- Location = Vila da Castanheira
- Dedicators = Unknown
- References = EE IX, 27; Tranoy 1981:317.

58. Jupiter Optimus Maximus
- '[I(ovi)] O(ptimo) [M(aximo) / ...] I? [.../ E]lp(idius) E[u]/elpistus / v(otum) s(oluit)' (AE 1983, 552).
- Location = Cerzedelo (Guimarâes).
- Dedicators = ...Elpistus
- References = AE 1983, 552; Tranoy 1981:317.

59. Jupiter Optimus Maximus
- '[E]x of(ficina) Elp[idi?] / [I(ovi) O(ptimo)] M[ax?(imo) / ...]' (AE 1983, 551).
- Location = S. Cruz de Lima (Ponte de Lima).
- Dedicators = Unknown
- References = AE 1983, 551; Tranoy 1981:31.

60. Jupiter Optimus Maximus
- '[I(ovi)?] O(ptimo) M(aximo) / sacr[um...]' (AE 1983, 550).
- Location = Ronfe
- Dedicators = Unknown
- References = AE 1983, 550; Tranoy 1981:317.

61. Jupiter Optimus Maximus
- 'I(ovi) O(ptimo) Max(imo), (AE 1983, 549).
- Location = Mondim, Panque (Barcelos).
- Dedicators = Unknown
- References = AE 1983, 549; Tranoy 1981:317.

62. • Jupiter Optimus Maximus
- Jupiter Optimus Maximus (Tranoy 1981:317)
- Location = Joane
- Dedicators = Unknown (Tranoy 1981:317).
- References = Tranoy 1981:317; Unpublished.

63. Jupiter Optimus Maximus
- 'Iovi / Opti/mo M/...' (CIL II 5566).
- Location = S. Faustino de Vizella (Vizella)
- Dedicators = Unknown
- References = CIL II 5566; Tranoy 1981:317; ILER 6.

64. Jupiter Optimus Maximus
- 'I(o)vi (O)pti/mo Mx/sumo' (CIL II 5565).
- Location = Cerzedelo, Guimarâes
- Dedicators = Unknown

- References = CIL II 5565; Tranoy 1981:318

65. Jupiter Optimus Maximus
- 'Iovi Op M/....../....../....../ votum' (CIL II 2386).
- Location = Ribalonga
- Dedicators = Unknown
- References = CIL II 2386; Tranoy 1981:318.

66. Jupiter Optimus Maximus
- 'M S Iov/ O M v/m' (CIL II 2385).
- Location = Marco de Canaveses
- Dedicators = Unknown (M.S?)
- References = CIL II 2385; Tranoy 1981:318.

67. Jupiter Optimus Maximus
- 'Iovi / O M / Fl(avius) Pr(oculus) (or P(rimus)) / IIIX vo/to lib' (AE 1962:238). ILER 120 has the dedicator as 'Fl. Fr(onto).'
- Location = S. Leocadia (Baiâo)
- Dedicators = Flavius Fronto
- References = Ramirez 1981:243; AE 1962, 238; Tranoy 1981:316; ILER 120.

68. Jupiter Optimus Maximus
- 'I.O.M./ Flavius Aven/tinus Encrati / uxori v.s.' (CIL II 2406).
- Location = Caldas de Vizela
- Dedicators = Flavius Aventinus
- References = CIL II 2406; Tranoy 1981:316; Ramirez 1981:243.

69. Jupiter Optimus Maximus
- '[Fl]avus Iov[i] / O(ptimo) M(aximo) v(otum) / m(erito)' (CIL II 5557).
- Location = S. Maria de Freixo (Caldas de Vizela)
- Dedicator = Flavus
- References = CIL II 5557.

70. Jupiter Optimus Maximus
- 'Iov(i) O(ptimo) M(aximo) / Flavia Materna / soluite vota' (Rodríguez Colmenero 1977:332).
- Location = Queizas
- Dedicators = Flavia Materna
- References = Rodríguez Colmenero 1977:332; Tranoy 1981:316; Ramirez 1981:242.

71. Jupiter Optimus Maximus
- 'Iovi Optim. M. / Alius Reburrus / redidi vot(u)m' (ILER 56).
- Location = Vilar de Maçada (Vila Real).
- Dedicators = Aelius Reburrus
- References = Ramirez 1981:242; CIL II 2394; ILER 56; Tranoy 1981:316.

72. Jupiter Optimus Maximus
- 'I(ovi) O(ptimo) M(aximo) / Val(erius) Rebu(r)rus sacrum / f(acendum) c(uravit)' (Rodríguez Colmenero 1977:333).
- Location = Tâmega river (Chaves).
- Dedicators = Valerius Reburrus
- References = Rodríguez Colmenero 1977:333; Tranoy 1981:316; Ramirez 1981:243.

73. Jupiter Optimus Maximus

- 'Iovi Op(timo) Ma/x(imo) ex de(creto) s(uo) / sacrum/ M(arcus) Philip(us) Ma(ximus) / posuit' (AE 1976, 297). Dedicator as 'M. Phillipus Maximus' in AE 1976, 297, Tranoy 1981:316, and in Rodríguez Colmenero 1977:332. 'Minipma' in IRG IV, 69 and ILER 65. Ramirez lists both options (1981:242).
- Location = Santiago de Trasariz (Chaves)
- Dedicators = M. Phillipus Maximus
- References = Rodríguez Colmenero 1977:332; Ramirez 1981:242; AE 1976, 297; IRG IV, 69; Tranoy 1981:316; ILER 65.

74. Jupiter Optimus Maximus
- 'I(ovi) O(ptimo) M(aximo) / Publius / Aelius / Flaccinus / v(otum) s(oluit) l(ibens) m(erito)' (Rodríguez Colmenero 1977:333).
- Location = Vale de Talhas
- Dedicators = P. Aelius Flaccinus
- References = Rodríguez Colmenero 1977:333; Tranoy 1981:316; Ramirez 1981:243; CIL II 2466.

75. Jupiter Optimus Maximus
- 'Iovi / Optimo / Maximo / Flavus / Corol/leae f / v.s.l.m' (CIL II 2376).
- Location = S. João de Pendorada (S. Martin de Varzea).
- Dedicators = Flavus, son of Corolla
- References = CIL II 2376; Tranoy 1981:316; Ramirez 1981:242.

76. Jupiter Optimus Maximus
- 'Iovi O(ptimo) / M(aximo) vot(um) / Titus / Albini r/etulit / libens / meritu / m(onumentum)' (IRG IV, 64).
- Location = Gresuxe (S. Juan de Crespos).
- Dedicators = Titus, son of Albinus
- References = IRG IV, 64; Tranoy 1981:317; Ramirez 1981:242; ILER 64.

77. Jupiter Optimus Maximus
- 'Iovi / O M / Loviis/(s)a iix / voto lap' (CIL II 2467).
- Location = Vinhais (Chaves)
- Dedicators = Lovesa
- References = CIL II 2467; Tranoy 1981:317; Ramirez 1981:243; ILER 146.

78. Jupiter Optimus Maximus
- 'Q(uintus) Annius / Modestus / m(iles) l(egionis) VII o(pus) p(onere) Iovi O(ptimo) M(aximo) c(urauit)' (Parente 1981:133).
- Location = Ribeirinha, Trêsminas
- Dedicator = Q. Annius Modestus, soldier of the legio VII.
- References = Parente 1980:133-4; AE 1980, 582.

79. Jupiter Optimus Maximus
- 'I(ovi) O(ptimo) M(aximo) / G. Iul(ius) Sa/turninus / mil(es) leg(inois) / VII Gem(inae) / F(elicis) // Afer' (AE 1993, 1025).
- Location = Braga
- Dedicator = G. Iulius Saturninus
- References = AE 1993, 1025.

80. Jupiter Optimus Maximus
- 'I(ovi) O(ptimo) M(aximo)' (AE 1990, 539).
- Location = Antela (Veiga de), Orense.
- Dedicator = Unsure
- References = AE 1990, 539.

81. Jupiter Optimus Maximus
- 'Iovi Op(timo) Ma(ximo) / vicani / Vagor/nicens/es sacru(m)' (AE 1982, 567).
- Location = Friâes, Valapaços.
- Dedicator = Unsure (the vicus Vagornica)
- References = AE 1982, 567.

82. Jupiter Optimus Maximus
- 'I(ovi) O(ptimo) M(aximo) / Valuti(us) / Paul(l)us / ex vo/to' (AE 1983:581).
- Location = Sta. Marinha, Ribeira de Pena (Vila Real).
- Dedicator = Valutius Paullus
- References = AE 1983:581; CIL II 2388.

83. Jupiter Optimus Maximus
- 'Icascaen / Tamagonum / Dec(urio) al(ae) Gic(urrorum) / comili(tones) …/ …/ Iovi O(ptimo) M(aximo) v(otum) s(olverunt) l(ibentes) m(erito)' (Pastor Muňoz 1976:499).
- Location = Castro de Cabanca, near Castrelo del Valle, (Verín), on the bank of the Tamega river (Orense).
- Dedicator = Icascaen Tamaognum, the indigenous Decurion of the the I. Ala Gigurrorum (Pastor Muňoz 1976:498).
- References = Pastor Muňoz 1976:498-9; IRG IV, 66; García y Bellido 1961:140.

84. Jupiter Optimus Maximus and the health of the Emperor
- Pro s(alute) / Ti(beri) C(laud?) Ni[s]g(ri or rini?) / I(ovi) O(ptimo) / M(aximo) / Hermes / v(otum) l(ibens) s(oluit)' (AE 1983, 553).
- Location = Esporôes
- Dedicators = Hermes
- References = AE 1983, 553; Tranoy 1981:317.

85. Jupiter Optimus Maximus and the health of Marcus Aurelius and Lucius Verus
- 'I(ovi) O(ptimo) M(aximo) / pro salute / M(arci) Aurelii Antonini / et Aureli Veri / Augustorum / --- / III idus Iunias / Laeliano et Pastore co(n)s(ulibus)' (IRG IV, 61).
- Location = Region of Laguna Antela or Lago Beón (Province of Orense).
- Dedicator = Unsure
- References = IRG IV, no.61.

86. Jupiter Optimus Maximus Conservator?
- 'Iovi / O(ptimo) M(aximo) C(onservator) (?)/ Colo/ticen(us) (?) // (to the left) of(ficina) Locusis (?)' (AE 1985, 574).
- Location = Sabrosa do Douro
- Dedicator = Coloticenus?
- References = AE 1985, 574.

87. Jupiter Optimus Maximus Municipalis
- 'I(upiter) O(ptimus) M(aximus) / Muni/cipalis' (AE 1973, 305).
- Location = Chaves
- Dedicators = Unknown
- References = AE 1973, 305; Tranoy 1981:316.

88. Lares Civitatis Limicorum

- First Face = '[L]ari(bus) civita[tis / Li]m(icorum) Claud(ius) / Taciu[s] / et Ta[pilus].' Second Face = 'Tapilus / Taciu[…] / v(otum) s(oluerunt)' (AE 1976, no.295). The decoration on this altar of an indigenous sacrifice scene is exceptional in the NW (Tranoy 1981:323).
- Location = Mont de San Pedro (Nocelo da Pena, Ginzo de Limia).
- Dedicators = Claudius Tacius and Tapilus
- References = AE 1976, no.295; Tranoy 1981:323; Ramirez 1981:247.

89. Lares Marini
- 'Larebus / Marini/s Ulpiu/s Flav(u)s / votum / solui[t]' (AE 1973, 311).
- Location = Porto
- Dedicator = Ulpius Flavus
- References = AE 1973, 311; Tranoy 1981:323; Alarcâo 1988, Vol.II:1/450.

90. Lar Patrius
- 'Lari patrio / Ladronius(?) / Avitis filius votum solu/it, propitius / sis rogo' (AE 1973, no.319).
- Location = Penafiel
- Dedicator = Ladronius, son of Avitis
- References = Tranoy 1981:322; Ramirez 1981:247; AE 1973, 319.

91. Lares Viales
- 'Val(erius) / Ruf(us) / Lar(ibus) v(ialibus) / p(osuit)' (AE 1983, 555).
- Location = Castelo de Nieva (Viana do Castelo)
- Dedicator = Valerius Rufus
- References = AE 1983, 555; Tranoy 1981:323.

92. Lares Viales
- 'Lari(bus) Vi/alibvs / Petro/nius / ex vo(to)' (AE 1974, 396).
- Location = Layoso (Orense)
- Dedicator = Petronius
- References = Ramirez 1981:246; AE 1974, 396.

93. Lares Viales
- 'Laribus / Vialibus / Mater/nus Rufi / l(ibens) a(nimo) p(osuit)' (AE 1973, 310).
- Location = Braga
- Dedicator = Maternus, son of Rufus
- References = Ramirez 1981:246; AE 1973, 310.

94. Lares Viales
- 'Larib . Viali/bus . Fl . Sa/binus . v/ s . l . m.' (CIL II 2417).
- Location = Braga
- Dedicator = Flavius Sabinus
- References = Ramirez 1981:246; CIL II 2417.

95. Lares Viales
- 'Maximus [L]ov/essi f(ilius) La\ribus Vi/alibus / v(otum) s(oluit) l(ibens) m(erito)'
- (IRG IV, 79).
- Location = Sta. Comba de Bande
- Dedicator = Maximus, son of Lovessus
- References = Ramirez 1981:246; IRG, IV, 79; ILER 583.

96. Mars
- 'Deo Marti / sacrum ……/……/……/……/……/ v.l.m.s' (CIL II 2463). Incomplete and now lost.
- Location = Viana do Castelo
- Dedicator = Unknown
- References = Ramirez 1981:244; Tranoy 1981:314; CIL II 2463; ILER 228.

97. Mars
- 'Marti' (Rodríguez Colmenero 1977:307). Altar in poor condition and difficult to read (Tranoy 1981:314).
- Location = Conserved in the chapel of San Roque a Espiño (Oimbra, Verín).
- Dedicator = Unsure.
- References = Rodríguez Colmenero 1977:307; Tranoy 1981:314.

98. • Mars
- 'Mars' (Difficult to read; the Mars is preceded by a 'D' standing for 'Deus' –Tranoy 1981:314).
- Location = Velle (Near Orense).
- Dedicator = C. [M?]arius Saturni[nus?], a tria-nomina
- References = Tranoy 1981:314; Unpublished.

99. Mars Victor
- 'Deo Marti Vic/tori . ob . ev/entum . bo/num . gladi/atori mun/eris / Ceraeci/us Fuscu/s ex / voto' (CIL II 2473).
- Location = Outeiro Seco (Chaves)
- Dedicator = Cereaeicius Fuscus ('Muneris' of gladiators).
- References = Ramirez 1981:244; CIL II 2473; ILER 227.

100. Mercury
- 'Merc/urio / ara(m) / Festus / f[e]cit' (CIRG II, no.138).
- Location = Planxón, Nigrán (Vigo).
- Dedicator = Festus
- References = CIRG II, no.138; Tranoy 1981:315; Ramirez 1981:245; AE 1969-70, 255; ILER 268.

101. Mercury
- 'Deo / Mer(curio) / Fro(nto) / Cap(ito) / ex v(oto) p(osuit)

(CIRG II, no.140).
- Location = San Vicente de Marzán (El Rosal, La Guardia, Pontevedra)
- Dedicator = Fronto Capito
- References = CIRG II, no.140; Tranoy 1981:315.

102. Mercury
- 'Mer[c]uri[o / …]' (AE 1983, 556).
- Location = Braga.
- Dedicator = Unsure
- References = AE 1983, 556.

103. Nymphs
- 'D(e)ab(us) Nymphis' (Alarcâo 1988, Vol.II:1/141).
- Location = Caldelas (Amarés).
- Dedicator = Unknown
- References = Alarcâo 1988, Vol. II:1/141; Tranoy 1981:325.

104. Nymphs
- 'Caen(i)cien(us) Nymphis ex voto' (Santos Junior & Cardozo 1953:60).
- Location = Caldelas (Amarés).
- Dedicator = Caenicienus/Caeniciena?
- References = Santos Junior & Cardozo 1953:60; Alarcâo 1988, Vol. II:1/141; Tranoy 1981:325.

105. Nymphs
- 'Nymphis / Calpurnia Abana / Aeboso / ex visu v(otum) s(oluit) l(ibens)' (IRG IV, 74).
- Location = Burgas de Orense (Orense)
- Dedicator = Calpurnia Abana Aeboso(ca) (Rodríguez Colmenero 1977:303).
- References = IRG IV, 74; Rodríguez Colmenero 1977:303; Ramirez 1981:244; Tranoy 1981:325; CIL II 2527; ILER 619.

106. Nymphs
- 'D(iis) (or Deabus) Nymphis v(otum) posuit Simplicia s(oluit) l(ibens) (animo)' (Santos Junior & Cardozo 1953:63).
- Location = Horta da Vilariça, Quinta do Carrascal, Concelho de Moncorvo, Trás-os-Montes
- Dedicator = Simplicia
- References = Santos Junior & Cardozo 1953:63; Tranoy 1981:325.

107. Nymphs
- 'Nymphis Aur(elius) Dionysius Aug(usti) lib(ertus)' (Santos Junior & Cardozo 1953:62).
- Location = Chaves
- Dedicator = Aurelius Dionysius, a freedman.
- References = Santos Junior & Cardozo 1953:62; Rodríguez Colmenero 1977:304; Tranoy 1981:325; Ramirez 1981:244; CIL II 2474; ILER 609.

108. Nymphs
- 'Urbanus pro Crysede Nymphis ex voto posui(t)' (Santos Junior & Cardozo 1953:60).
- Location = Guimarâes
- Dedicators = Urbinus, for Crysedis
- References = Santos Junior & Cardozo 1953:60; Alarcâo 1988, Vol. II:1/302; CIL II 5569; ILER 606; Tranoy 1981:325.

109. Nymphs
- 'Nymphis G(allus) Sulp(icius) Festus ex voto' (Santos Junior & Cardozo 1953:63).
- Location = S. Joâo de Ponte (Guimarâes)
- Dedicator = G. Sulpicius Festus
- References = Tranoy 1981:325; Alarcâo 1988, Vol. II:1/260; Santos Junior & Cardozo 1953:63.

110. Nymphs
- 'Aurelius / Flavs / Tamacanus / Nymphis / ex voto' (Rodríguez Colmenero 1977:303). 'Tanstacanus' in Tranoy, which he suggests reflects an indigenous ethnic group. 'T(r)anstaganus' in IRG IV, 76. Blázquez translates 'Tanitacuae,' and proposes this to be a surname for the Nymphs (1962:190).
- Location = Sta. Eufemia de Ambia (Orense)
- Dedicator = Aurelius Flavus Tamacanus.
- References = Rodríguez Colmenero 1977:303; Tranoy 1981:325; Ramirez 1981:244; Blázquez 1962:190; IRG IV, 76.

111. Nymphs
- 'Nym(hi)S / Boeli/us Ruf/us pro / salute / s[ua] v(otum) s(oluit)' (IRG IV, 75).
- Location = S. Juan de Baños de Bande
- Dedicator = Boelius Rufus
- References = IRG IV, 75; Tranoy 1981:325; Ramirez 1981:244; CIL II 2530; Rodríguez Colmenero 1977:302-3; ILER 611.

112. Nymphs (Marinas)
- 'Nym(phis) Mari(nis) / Ac(cilius?) Ca(tulus?) / Ast(uricae) Aug(ustae) / v(otum) s(oluit) l(ibens) m(erito)' (IRG IV, 78).
- Location = S. Miguel de Canedo (Orense).
- Dedicator = Ac(ilius) Ca(tulus)? An inhabitant of Astorga.
- References = IRG IV, 78; Rodríguez Colmenero 1977:303-4; Tranoy 1981:324; Pastor Muňoz 1976:522; Ramirez 1981:244.

113. Nymphae Salutales
- 'Nymphis / Salut(is) lib(ens) Sulpicia / Saturni/na. ex./ voto.' (Rodríguez Colmenero 1977:304).
- Location = Bóveda (Amoeiro, Orense). Near the ancient spring 'Fonte das Lameiras.'
- Dedicator = Sulpicia Saturninia
- References = Rodríguez Colmenero 1977:304; Tranoy 1981:325; Ramirez 1981:244; AE 1974, 397.

114. Serapis with Destiny and the Mysteries
- Υψίστω Σεrά/πιδι συν γάστ/ρα χαι μυστα/ρίοις G . C. Calp(urnius) / Rufinus u(ir) c(larissimus)' (AE 1997, 860).
- Location = Santuary of Panóias, (Assentos, Vale de Nogueira, Vila Real).
- Dedicator = G.C. Calpurnius Rufinus
- References = AE 1997, 860; CIL II 2395c; Rodríguez Colmenero 1993:65-7; Tranoy 1981:336; Alarcâo 1988:Vol.II,1/386.

115. Sol
- 'Soli' (AE 1981,534).
- Location = S. Salvador de Arnoia, Orense.
- Dedicator = Unsure
- References = AE 1981, 534; Tranoy 1981:312

116. Tellus
- 'Telluri / G(aius) Sulp(icius) / Flavus / ex voto' (IRG IV, 73).
- Location = Orense
- Dedicator = G. Sulpicius Flavus
- References = Tranoy 1981:312; CIL II 2526; IRG IV, 73; Rodríguez Colmenero 1977:295; ILER 647.

117. Tutela
- 'Tutelae / M . Aq . Leda/ peregrinorum / ex v. p' (CIL II 5618).
- Location = Chaves
- Dedicator = M. Aq. Leda (a foreigner)
- References = Ramirez 1981:245; Tranoy 1981:322; CIL II 5618; ILER 482.

118. Tutela
- 'Tutelae . . . e . . .tius Ca. . .s v. s(oluit) l(ibens) m(erito)' (Rodríguez Colmenero 1977:335).
- Location = S. Tome (Orense)
- Dedicator = Unsure.
- References = Rodríguez Colmenero 1977:335; Tranoy 1981:322.

119. Venus Victrix
- 'Veneri / Victric / l(ibens) a(nimo) ex vi(su) / ar(am) p(osuit)' (AE 1933, 23). Rodríguez Colmenero has: 'Veneri / Victrici L(ucius) A(ntonius) (hedera) ex vi(su) / ar(am) p(osuit)' (1977:334).
- Location = Aquae Flaviae (Chaves)
- Dedicator = Unsure. Rodríguez Colmenero has 'Lucius Antonius' (1977:334).
- References = Rodríguez Colmenero 1977:334; Tranoy 1981:312; Ramirez 1981:245; AE 1933, 23; ILER 415.

Uncertain Reading from the Conventus Bracaraugustanus

120. Mars/Matres?
- '……/ pro salut(e) / [I]uliae Au/g(ustae) Matri / Castror(um) et Aug(ust)o(ru)m / Didius M/arinus / [P]r(aefectus) OO (cohortis) di/cauit' (IRG IV, 102). May be to 'Marti' – see for example the Mar Gravidus altar with the same dedicator.
- Location = Sta. Comba de Bande
- Dedicator = Didius Marinus
- References = Ramirez 1981:244; IRG, IV, 102; CIL II 2529.

Conventus Lucensis

121. All gods and Apollo Clarius
- 'Dis D(eabus)q(ue) / ex int(e)rp/retation(e) / oraculi / Clari Apo/[l]linis C[.] / A D sacr-/v[m –c.6-]' (CIRG I, no.60).
- Location = Chapel of Sta. Eulalia de Portorroibo, As Pontes, La Coruña.
- Dedicator = Unsure
- References = CIRG I, no.60; AE 1990, 545.

122. Caelestis Augusta
- 'Caelesti / Aug(ustae) / Paterni / qui et / Constantii / vv(ota) ss(oluerunt)' (Arias Vilas, Le Roux & Tranoy 1979:no.1).
- Location = Lugo
- Dedicators = The Paterni and the Constantii
- References = Arias Vilas, Le Roux & Tranoy 1979:no.1; Tranoy 1981:310, Ramirez 1981:245; CIL II 2570; IRG II, 68; ILER 322.

123. Cautes
- 'Cau/ti/ nto / ….' (CIL II 5635).
- Location = Caldas de Reyes
- Dedicator = Unsure
- References = CIL II 5635; Tranoy 1981:335.

124. Cybele
- 'Matri De/um s(acrum) + (---) / et Val(---) e(x) / voto' (CIRG I, no.71). But, ILER 980 has lines 1-2: 'Mard/umus.'
- Location = Sardiñeiro (Fisterra)
- Dedicator = Val(---)
- References = CIRG I, no.71; ILER 980.

125. Diana
- 'Dian(a)e / sacr(um) / s p l d / [ex] v(oto) / ------.' (CIRG II, no.88).
- Location = Moimenta (Lalín, Pontevedra).
- Dedicator = Unknown.
- References = Tranoy 1981:313; Ramirez 1981:244; IRG III, 19; ILER 336.

126. Diana Venatrix
- 'Dian(a)e / Venat/rici ar(am) / po(suerunt) Ur(sus) / et Faustinus / ex pr(aecepto) / Victori/s pro s/a(lute) sua' (CIRG I, no.76). In Tranoy: 'Uretius' (1981:313). CIL II 5638 puts: 'Arpo Urei (filius) Faustanus,' but IRG III, 18 puts: 'Ar(am) po(suit) Uret(inus) Faustinus.' ILER 334 has: 'Urcet. Faustinus' as the dedicator.
- Location = Porto Són (La Coruña).
- Dedicator = Ursus and Faustinus
- References = CIRG I, no.76; Tranoy 1981:313; Ramirez 1981:244; CIL II 5638; IRG III, 18; ILER 334.

127. Fortuna
- 'Fort/unae / Iulius / Plato / ex vo(to)' (CIRG I, no.1).
- Location = La Coruña
- Dedicator = Iulius Plato
- References = CIRG I, no.1; Tranoy 1981:321; Ramirez 1981:245; CIL II 2558; ILER 439.

128. Fortuna
- 'Fortun/ae M(arcus) Se(---) / Agaton / ex v(oto)' (CIRG I, no.40).
- Location = Brandomil (La Coruña).
- Dedicator = M. Se(mpronius?) Agaton
- References = CIRG I, no.40; AE 1982, 570; Tranoy 1981:321.

129. Fortuna
- 'Fortu/n(a)e Val(erius) / Lupus / opt(io) / v(otum) s(oluit) l(ibens) m(erito)' (CIRG I, no.31).
- Location = Found in situ in the Roman camp of Cidadela (CIRG I, no.31). At Sobrado dos Monxes, La Coruña.
- Dedicator = Valerius Lupus, an optio of the cohort I Celtiberorum (CIRG I, no.31).
- References = CIRG I, no.31; AE 1986, 387.

130. Jupiter
- 'R(ufinus) Bassi/anus v/otum / Iovi / l(ibens) a(nimo) s(oluit)' (CIRG I, no.62).
- Location = San Vicente de Fervenzas (Aranga).
- Dedicator = R(ufinus) Bassianus
- References = CIRG I, no.62.

131. Jupiter
- 'I(ovi) [---] / a + [---] / + PE ex / voto' (CIRG I, no.64 – suggests it may be: 'I(ovi) [O(ptimo) M(aximo)] / a[ram po(suit) or similar] / [name of dedicator abbreviated] ex / voto').
- Location = Uncertain (Lucensis)
- Dedicator = Unsure
- References = CIRG I, no.64; Otherwise unpublished.

132. Jupiter
- 'Iovi / ex vot(o) / P(ublius) Ant(onius)' (ERA, no.3).
- Location = Boal
- Dedicator = Publius Antonius (?)
- References = ERA, no.3; Pastor Muñoz 1976:495; Tranoy 1981:318; CIL II 2692; ILER 74.

133. Jupiter Optimus Maximus
- 'Iovi / O(ptimo) Ma(ximo) / a(ram) p(osuit) P(---) / Ma(---) p(ro) s(alute) / s(ua)' (CIRG I, no.84).
- Location = Uncertain (Lucense)
- Dedicators = Unsure (A.P.P.MA.P.S.S.)
- References = CIRG I, no.84; Tranoy 1981:318; IRG, I, 3.

134. Jupiter Optimus Maximus
- 'I(ovi) O(ptimo) M(aximo) / (Castellum) Au/iliob/ris pr(o) s(alute)' (CIRG I, no.66).
- Location = Cores (Ponteceso)
- Dedicators = The Castellum Auiliober
- References = CIRG I, no.66; AE 1992, 997; Tranoy 1981:316.

135. Jupiter Optimus Maximus
- 'Iovi / Op(timo) Ma(ximo) / Ma(---)' (CIRG I, no.24).
- Location = In a church in Sta. Eulalia de Logrosa, (Negreira)
- Dedicators = Ma(ximus?)
- References = CIRG I, no.24; Tranoy 1981:318; CIL II 5641; ILER 3.

136. Jupiter Optimus Maximus
- 'I(ovi) O(ptimo) M(aximo) / a(ram) p(osuit) s(ua) p(ecunia) / S(---) M(---)' (CIRG I, no.23).
- Location = In a church in Sta. Eulalia de Logrosa, (Negreira)
- Dedicators = Unsure (S…M…?).
- References = CIRG I, no.23; Tranoy 1981:318; CIL II 5640; ILER 34.

137. Jupiter Optimus Maximus
- 'Iovi / O(ptimo) M(aximo)' (CIRG I, no.19).
- Location = S. Pedro de Herbogo (Rois, 7km NE of Padrón).
- Dedicators = Unsure
- References = CIRG I, no.19; Tranoy 1981:318.

138. Jupiter Optimus Maximus
- 'Io[vi] / Optu/mo Max/umo / a(ram) p(osuit) T(itus) Li/rcin(us?)' (CIRG II, no.100). Tranoy has 'Rufinus' as the dedicator (1981:318).
- Location = Cesures, Pontevedra
- Dedicators = Titus Lircinus ?
- References = CIRG II, no.100; Tranoy 1981:317; IRG, III, 15; Ramirez 1981:242: ILER 37.

139. Jupiter Optimus Maximus
- 'I.O.M. / Flacci/nius M/ … / …' (ILER 81).
- Location = Santiago de Compostela
- Dedicator = Flaccinus
- References = Tranoy 1981:317; Ramirez 1981:242; ILER 81.

140. Jupiter Optimus Maximus
- 'Iovi / Opt . Max / Q . Pu////// Dion(y)sius / ex voto' (CIL II 2537).
- Location = Santiago de Aranza
- Dedicator = Q. Pu(blius) Dionysius (Freedman)
- References = CIL II 2537; Tranoy 1981:316; Ramirez 1981:242.

141. Jupiter Optimus Maximus
- 'Sulp(icius) / Cleme/ns iu(ssu) e(ius) / Iovi O(ptimo) M(aximo) / v(otum) s(oluit) l(ibens) m(erito)' (Arias Vilas, Le Roux & Tranoy 1979:no.3).
- Location = Lugo
- Dedicator = Sulpicius Clemens
- References = Arias Vilas, Le Roux & Tranoy 1979:no.3; Tranoy 1981:316; CIL II 2571; IRG II, 5; ILER 133.

142. Jupiter Optimus Maximus
- 'Iovi / Op(timo) Ma/x(imo) Fla(vius) / Flavus / [e]x vo/to' (Arias Vilas, Le Roux & Tranoy 1979:no.2).
- Location = Lugo
- Dedicator = Flavius Flavus
- References = Arias Vilas, Le Roux & Tranoy 1979:no.2; Tranoy 1981:317; CIL II 5644; IRG II, 4; ILER 13.

143. Jupiter Optimus Maximus
- 'I(ovi) O(ptimo) M(aximo) Herculi Tongo s(oluit) v(otum)' (IRG I, 4).
- Location = The church of San Pedro de Soandres.
- Dedicator = Tongo, son of Hercules(?)
- References = IRG I, 4; ILER 78.

144. Jupiter Optimus Maximus Conservator
- 'I(ovi) O(ptimo) M(aximo) / Conserva/tori M(arcus) Aur(elius) / Severus / votum / s(oluit) l(ibens) m(erito)' (Arias Vilas, Le Roux & Tranoy 1979:no.4).
- Location = Lugo
- Dedicator = Marcus Aurelius Severus
- References = Arias Vilas, Le Roux & Tranoy 1979:no.4; Tranoy 1981:316; IRG II, 3; ILER 97.

145. Lares Viales
- 'Lari/bus / Vial(ibus)' (Arias Vilas, Le Roux & Tranoy 1979:no.60).
- Location = Belesar (Chantada)
- Dedicator = Unknown
- References = Arias Vilas, Le Roux & Tranoy 1979:no.60; Ramirez 1981:246; IRG II, 8; ILER 579.

146. Lares Viales
- 'Lari(bus) / Vial(ibus) / ex vo(to)' (Arias Vilas, Le Roux & Tranoy 1979:no.61).
- Location = Bouzoá, Arcos (Pol).
- Dedicator = Unknown
- References = Arias Vilas, Le Roux & Tranoy 1979:no.61; Ramirez 1981:246; IRG, II, 9; ILER 581.

147. Lares Viales
- 'Laribu[s] / Vialib(us) / Placid[i]na ex v/oto p[o]/suit' (Arias Vilas, Le Roux & Tranoy 1979:no.62).
- Location = Papín, Penarrubia (Baralla).

- Dedicator = Placidina
- References = Arias Vilas, Le Roux & Tranoy 1979:no.62; Ramirez 1981:246; IRG, II, 10; ILER 582.

148. Lares Viales
- 'Larib[us] / Via[libus] / Iuliu[s] / v(otum) s(oluit) [l(ibens) m(erito)]' (Arias Vilas, Le Roux & Tranoy 1979:no.63).
- Location = San Vicente de Castillós (Ferreira de Pantón).
- Dedicator = Julius
- References = Arias Vilas, Le Roux & Tranoy 1979:no.63; Ramirez 1981:246.

149. Lares Viales
- 'Larebus / Vialebus / Cl(audius?) Gauce / Ascrier/us Veren(i filius ou sis?)' (Arias Vilas, Le Roux & Tranoy 1979:no.64).
- Location = San Vicente de Castillós (Pantón).
- Dedicator = Claudius Gauce Ascrierus, son of Verenus (or of 'Verensis').
- References = Arias Vilas, Le Roux & Tranoy 1979:no.64; Ramirez 1981:246.

150. Lares Viales
- 'Lare/bus V/ealib/us a(ram) s(ua) p(ecunia) / S(everius or –ulpicius) e(x) v(oto) p(osuit)' (Arias Vilas, Le Roux & Tranoy 1979:no.65).
- Location = San Pedro de Buriz, A Graña (Guitiriz).
- Dedicator = S…?
- References = Arias Vilas, Le Roux & Tranoy 1979:no.65; Ramirez 1981:246.

151. Lares Viales
- 'Laribus / Vialibus Caes[i]/anus' (Arias Vilas, Le Roux & Tranoy 1979:no.66).
- Location = Santa Cruz de Parga (Guitiriz).
- Dedicator = Caesianus
- References = Arias Vilas, Le Roux & Tranoy 1979:no.66; Ramirez 1981:246.

152. Lares Viales
- '[---] Rec[---] / [---]us Ge[---] / [La]ribu[s---] / [V]ial[i]b[us---]' (CIRG II, no.75).
- Location = Caldas de Reyes (Pontevedra)
- Dedicator = Rectus …?
- References = CIRG II, no.75; Ramirez 1981:246; IRG, III, 23.

153. Lares Viales
- 'S(---) Lupus / vo(tum) s(oluit) l(ibens) / Laribvs / Vialibvs' (CIRG II, no.101). ILER 586 has: 'S. Lutu[s]' as the dedicator.
- Location = Pontecesures
- Dedicator = S. Lupus
- References = CIRG II, no.101; Ramirez 1981:246; IRG, III, 22; ILER 586.

154. Lares Viales
- 'Laribus / Vialibus / ara(m) Pu/blius O/ptatius / v(otum) s(oluit) l(ibens) m(erito)' (CIRG II, no.121).
- Location = Grava, Silleda (Pontevedra)
- Dedicator = Publius Optatius
- References = CIRG II, no.121; Ramirez 1981:246; IRG, III, 24; ILER 587.

155. Lares Viales
- '[L]aribus / [V]ialibus / [-c.2-] V [-c.3-]' (CIRG II, no.109). In IRG, III, 25: '[L]aribvs / Vialibus / a(ram) v(oto) s(oluit).'
- Location = Catoira (Pontevedra)
- Dedicator = Unknown
- References = CIRG II, no.109; Ramirez 1981:246; IRG, III, 25.

156. Lares Viales
- '[L]arib[u]/s V(ialibus) p(uella) / ar(am) p(osuit) / l(ibens) m(erito)' (IRG III, 26).
- Location = S. Andrés de Geve (Pontevedra)
- Dedicator = Unknown (a girl ?).
- References = Ramirez 1981:246; IRG, III, 26; ILER 589.

157. Lares Viales
- 'Laribus / [V]ialibus / Denton/ius Vere/cundus / v(otum) s(oluit) l(ibens) a(nimo)' (CIRG I, no.41).
- Location = Brandomil
- Dedicator = Dentonius Verecundus
- References = Ramirez 1981:246; IRG, I, 6; CIRG I, no.41; ILER 580.

158. Lares Viales
- 'L(aribus) V(ialibus) / Val (erius) O/[..]++ / ------' (CIRG I, no.57 – Only top fragment remains).
- Location = Castrofeito, O Pino
- Dedicator = Val(erius?)
- References = CIRG I, no.57; Otherwise unpublished

159. Lares Viales
- 'Laribus / Vialibus / ara(m) po/su(it) M[…]' (AE 1981, 539).
- Location = Temes, Carballedo, Lugo.
- Dedicator = Unsure
- References = AE 1981, 539.

160. Lares Viales and Two Augustii
- 'Augg(ustis doubus) sa/crum Laribus / Vialib(us) M M(arcii) / Anni Verus / et Verianus / cc (centurions) l[e]gg(ionum duarum) pa/ter et filius / ex voto' (Arias Vilas, Le Roux & Tranoy 1979:no.22). ILER 593 has: 'Aug(usti) Lar(ibus) sa/crum . . Laribus / Vialib. M. M/annius Varus / veteranus / ducenarius legionis (VII g(em) pa/ter et filius / ex voto.'
- Location = Lugo
- Dedicators = M. Annius Verus and M. Annius Verianus (father and son)
- References = Arias Vilas, Le Roux & Tranoy 1979:no.22; Tranoy 1981:324; IRG II, 11; AE 1973, 293; CIL II 2572; ILER 593.

161. Mars Augustus
- 'Marti/ Aug(usto) sacr(um) / G(aius) Sevius / Lupus / architectus / Aeminiensis / Lusitanus ex vo(to)' (CIRG I, no.2).
- Location = La Coruña
- Dedicator = Gaius Servius Lupus Aeminiensis Lusitanus (an architect from Coimbra)
- References = CIRG I, no.2; Tranoy 1981:314; Ramirez 1981:244; CIL II 2559; Rodríguez Colmenero 1993:96-9; ILER 250.

162. Mercury
- 'Deo M/ercu/rio Fu/scus / Fusci (filius) / v(otum) m(erito)

l(ibens) a(nimo)' (CIRG II, no.122).
- Location = Caldas de Reyes
- Dedicator = Fuscus, son of Fuscus
- References = CIRG II, no.122; Tranoy 1981:315; Ramirez 1981:245; CIL II 2544; ILER 267.

163. Mercury
- 'Mer/curio / Seve/rus / pro / vo/to' (CIRG II, no.122). Engraved on a great pillar in the indigenous tradition (Tranoy 1981:315).
- Location = Puente Cesures, Pontevedra.
- Dedicator = Severus
- References = CIRG II, no.122; Tranoy 1981:315; Ramirez 1981:245; AE 1969-70, 256; ILER 269.

164. Mercury
- 'Sacrum / Mercurio / …' (Arias Vilas, Le Roux & Tranoy 1979:no.69).
- Location = San Mamed de Oleiros (Villalba).
- Dedicator = Unknown.
- References = Tranoy 1981:315; Arias Vilas, Le Roux & Tranoy 1979:no.69; Ramirez 1981:245.

165. Mercury
- 'Maxu/mus S/ecundi (filius) vot(um) s(oluit) Mer(curio) me(rito)' (Arias Vilas, Le Roux & Tranoy 1979:no.70). In IRG II 24: 'Mer(itissi)me.' ILER 984 just has 'Mer.' which they do not interpret as Mercury.
- Location = As Virtudes, Adai (O Corgo).
- Dedicator = Maxumus, son of Secundus
- References = Arias Vilas, Le Roux & Tranoy 1979:no.70; Ramirez 1981:245; Tranoy 1981:315; IRG II 24; ILER 984.

166. Neptune
- 'Nep/tun(o) / sac(rum) / Q(---) C(---) / e(x) v(oto) / l(ibens) p(osuit)' (CIRG II, no.126). In IRG III,17: 'Q(unitus) C/eli(us)' for lines 4-5, and in ILER 294 'Q(uintus) C/el' for lines 4-5.
- Location = Villagarcía de Arosa (Northern Pontevedra Province).
- Dedicator = Q. C. (Quintus Celius?)
- References = CIRG II, no.126; Ramirez 1981:244; Tranoy 1981:312; IRG III,17; ILER 294.

167. Neptune
- 'Nept/uno / For(o)i(ri)-/e(n)ses / d(e) s(uo) p(osuerunt)' (CIRG I, no.12 – Read in various ways as it is difficult to decipher).
- Loc = Church of Santiago, Padrón.
- Dedicator = The Foroirienses (CIRG I, no.12).
- References = CIRG I, no.12; CIL II 2540.

168. Neptune and the health of the Emperor
- 'Neptuno / sacru[m]/ pro salute / Augustor(um) / nostror(um) / Gaucus / Caesar(um) n(ostrorum) / s(ervus) titul(um) / ex voto' (CIRG I, no.3). ILER 295 has: 'Neptuno / sacrum / pro salute / Augustor. / nostr. / Glaucus / Caesaris v(erna) / s. p. h(oc) s(oluit) l. // ex voto.'
- Location = La Coruña
- Dedicator = Gaucus
- References = CIRG I, no.3; Ramirez 1981:244; Tranoy 1981:312; ILER 295.

169. Nymphs
- 'Nymp/his C(aius) A/ntonius / Florus' (CIRG II, no.124).
- Location = Cuntis (Pontevedra)
- Dedicator = C. Antonius Florus
- References = CIRG II, no.124; Tranoy 1981:324; Ramirez 1981:244; IRG III, 20; CIL II 2546; ILER 603.

170. Nymphs
- 'Nymp/his C(aius) [A]ntonius / Florus' (CIRG II, no.125).
- Location = Cuntis (Pontevedra)
- Dedicator = C. Antonius Florus
- References = CIRG II, no.125; Tranoy 1981:324; Ramirez 1981:244; IRG III, 21.

171. Nymphs
- 'Rebur/rius Ter/tius Ny/mfis ex / voto' (CIRG I, no.38).
- Location = S. Vicente de Présares (Vilasantar, La Coruña).
- Dedicator = Reburrius Tertius
- References = CIRG I, no.38; Tranoy 1981:324; Ramirez 1981:244; ILER 607.

172. Nymphs
- Nymphis / M. Vlp(ius) Lon/ginianus / -------' (AE 2000, 749). Part of a bath complex. This altar was found with others to the Nymphs; on five of these the deity name can no longer be read but they appear to have been votive dedications as well (see AE 2000, 749-759).
- Location = Lugo
- Dedicator = M. Ulpius Longinianus
- References = AE 2000, 749; Herves Raigoso & Meijide Cameselle 2000:189.

173. Nymphs
- 'Nymphis / L. Val(erius) M[---] / ------' (AE 2000, 750).
- Location = Lugo
- Dedicator = L. Valerius M(---)
- References = AE 2000, 750; Herves Raigoso & Meijide Cameselle 2000:190.

174. Nymphs
- 'Nymphis / [---]E + V[---] / ------' (AE 2000, 751).
- Location = Lugo
- Dedicator = Unsure
- References = AE 2000, 751; Herves Raigoso & Meijide Cameselle 2000:190.

175. Nymphs
- 'Nymp[his] / sac[rum] / ------' (AE 2000, 752).
- Location = Lugo
- Dedicator = Unsure
- References = AE 2000, 752; Herves Raigoso & Meijide Cameselle 2000:190.

176. Nymphs
- 'Nym(phis) ? / ------' (AE 2000, 758).
- Location = Lugo
- Dedicator = Unsure
- References = AE 2000, 758; Herves Raigoso & Meijide Cameselle 2000:191.

177. Nymphs
- 'Nym(phis) ? / ------' (AE 2000, 759).
- Location = Lugo
- Dedicator = Unsure
- References = AE 2000, 759; Herves Raigoso & Meijide Cameselle 2000:191.

178. Pietas
- '[P]ietati Su/[-c.3-]+ C(---) Sev/[-c.5-]+ V/------' (CIRG II, no.110).
- Location = Catoira
- Dedicator = Unsure
- References = CIRG II, no.111; Otherwise unpublished.

179. Pietas
- 'Pietati / [-] Iunius / Flaccus / veteranu(s) leg(ionis) VII G(eminae) / v(otum) s(oluit) l(ibens) m(erito)' (CIRG I, no.51).
- Location = Vilar (Ames, La Coruña).
- Dedicator = Flaccus, veteranus of the Legio VII Gemina
- References = CIRG I, no.51; AE 1992, 996.

180. Sol Invictus (Mithras?)
- 'Deo / Invicto / Soli M/[ithrae?] / -------' (CIRG I, no.85).
- Location = Santiago
- Dedicator = Unknown
- References = CIRG I, no.85; IRG I, no.5; Tranoy 1981:335; ILER 292.

181. Tutela
- 'Tutel[ae / S]ilon(ius) [......?] / v(otum) [s(olvit) l(ibens) m(erito)]' (Arias Vilas, Le Roux & Tranoy 1979:no.10.).
- Location = Lugo
- Dedicator = Silonius ?
- References = Arias Vilas, Le Roux & Tranoy 1979:no.10; Tranoy 1981:322.

182. Venus Victirx, Africae Caelesti, Frugifer, Augusta Emerita and the Lares Callaecies (as well as probably I.O.M, the Numina Augusta, Juno Regina)
- '[Iovi Optimo Max(imo) ? / Numi]ni[b(us) Augu]stor(um) / [Iunoni R]e[gi]nae / Veneri Victrici / Africae Caelesti / Frugifero / Augustae Emeritae / et Larib(us) Callaeciar(um) / [S]aturninus Aug(usti) lib(ertus)' (Arias Vilas, Le Roux & Tranoy 1979:no.23).
- Location = Lugo
- Dedicator = Saturninus, freedman of Augustus.
- References = Arias Vilas, Le Roux & Tranoy 1979:no.23; AE 1973, no.294; Tranoy 1981:310.

Unsure Readings from the Conventus Lucense

183. L(ares) V(iales)?
- 'L V[.] / d s[.] / A L + / v p s' (CIRG II, no.117- which they propose translates as: 'L(airbus) V(ialibus) or V[i](alibus) / d(e) s(ua) [p(ecunia)] / A L+ (= dedicator's name)/ v(oto) p(o)s(uit).'
- Location = Found in the Necropolis of Adro Vello, San Vicente, O Grove.
- Dedicator = Unsure (A L?).
- References = CIRG II, no.117; Otherwise unpublished.

184. Lares Viales?
- '[L(aribus) Vi]ale(bus) / Arc (---) / v(oto) p(osuit) or p(osuerunt)' (CIRG I, no.58).
- Loc = Uncertain location in the Conventus Lucense
- Dedicator = Unsure (Arc....)
- References = CIRG I, no.58; Otherwise unpublished.

Conventus Asturum

185. (A)esculapius and Salus along with Serapis and Isis
- '(A)esculapio / Saluti / Serapidi / Isidi / L(ucius) Cassius Paulus / Augustanus Alpinus / Bellicus Sollers / et M(arcius) Sanctus Paullinus / Augustanus Alpinu(s)' (Pastor Muñoz 1976:500).
- Location = León
- Dedicators = L. Cassius Paullus Augustanus Alpinus Ballicus Sollers and M. Cassius Agrippa Sanctus Paullinus Augustanius Alpinus (both from Gaul) (Tranoy 1981:310).
- References = Tranoy 1981:310; Pastor Muñoz 1976:500-1; AE 1967, 223; ILER 189.

186. Apollo
- 'Apolini / sacrum / dumus / sacratus' (AE 1988, 761). Pastor Muñoz (1976:502) has: 'dumum.'
- Location = The ancient site of Lancia (Villasabariego, León).
- Dedicator = Unknown
- References = AE 1988, 761; Tranoy 1981:310; Pastor Muñoz 1976:502; HE 1989, no.416; ILER 165.

187. Apollo
- '... io Apolini' (Pastor Muñoz 1976:502).
- Location = Ponferrada
- Dedicator = Unknown.
- References = Tranoy 1981:310; Pastor Muñoz 1976:502; HE 1989, no.398.

188. Buena Fortuna (/Tyche) and Nemesis (of Smyrna)
- 'ΑΤΑ□□ ΤΥΧΗ / □ΕΑΙC ΝΕΜΕCΕΟΝ / ΖΜΥΡΝΑΙΑΙ CΕΒΑC ΙΩΤΑΤΑΙC / ΙΟΥΛ ΣΙΛVΑΝΟC / ΜΕΛΑΝΙΩΝ / ΕΠΤΡ. CΕΒ. ΕΥΧΗΝ' (Pastor Muñoz 1976:505).
- Location = Astorga
- Dedicator = Julius Silvanus Melanio (Procurator Augusti).
- References = Pastor Muñoz 1976:505; Tranoy 1981:321; Mañanez Perez 1982:no.4.

189. Camenius
- 'Camenio / Granius / Sabinus / leg(atus) Aug(usti)' (Quintana Prieto 1969:45).
- Location = From the site of Bergidum Flavium (castro of Ventosa) (near Sorribas and Cacebelos).
- Dedicator = The juridical legate Granius Sabinus.
- References = Quintana Prieto 1969:45-6; Tranoy 1981:310; AE 1962, no.243.

190. Diana
- First inscription = 'Dianae / sacrum / Q. Tullius / Maximus / leg. Aug / leg VII Gem / Felicis.' Second inscription = 'Aequora conclusit campi/ divisque dicauit / et templum statuit tibi / Delia virgo triformis / Tullius e Libya rector / legionis Hibernae / ut quiret volucris capreas / ut figere cervos / saetigeros ut apros ut/ equorum silvicolentum / progeniem ut cursu certare / ut disice ferri / et pedes arma gerens et / equo iaculator Hibero.' Third inscription = 'Dentes aprorum / quos cecidit / Maximus / dicat Dianae / pulchrum vir/tutis decus.' Fourth inscription = 'Cervom altifron/tum cornua / dicat Dianae / Tullius / quos vicit in pa/rami aequore / vectus feroci / sonipede.' Fifth inscription = 'Donat hac pelli D[iana] / Tullius te Maxim[us] / rector Aeneadum [vocamen?] / legio quis est se[ptima] / ipsa quam detrax[it urso?] / laude opima p[raeditus?]' (CIL 2660a-e). A great marble stela engraved with five inscriptions (3 are metric), consecrated to Diana (Pastor Muñoz 1976:503-4).
- Location = León
- Dedicator = Q. Tullius Maximus, Legate of the Legio VII Gemina between AD 162-6.

- References = Tranoy 1981:313-4; Pastor Muñoz 1976:503-4; CIL II 2660a-e; ILER 5754.

191. Diana
- '[Sa]nctae / [Dian]ae Ti. Iun(ius) / [Ti. f.] Quiri(na) / [Qu]adratus / [dom]o Roma / -----' (AE 1995, 857).
- Location = Petauonium (Rosinos de Vidriales), camp of Alae II Flavienne.
- Dedicator = Ti. Iunius Ti(?)
- References = AE 1995, 857.

192. Diana
- 'Dianae Aug(ustae) / [. A]rrius / [Co]nstans / Speratianus / praef(ectus) eq(uitum) sign(ifer) / uenator lib(rarius) ex [v]ot(o) / posuit' (AE 1995, 858).
- Location = Near Petauonium
- Dedicator = Arrius Constans Speratianus, praefectus equitum
- References = AE 1995, 858.

193. Dii (all gods) and the health of the Emperor Commodus
- 'Dis Deabusque / quos ius fasque est / precari in pantheo / P(ublius) Ael(ius) P. F. Hilarianus / proc(urator) Aug(usti) cum liberis / pro salute…/ Aug(usti)…' (Pastor Muñoz 1976:524).
- Location = Astorga
- Dedicator = P. Aelius Hilarianus (Procurator).
- References = Tranoy 1981:311; Pastor Muñoz 1976:524; Mañanez Perez 1982:no.2; AE 1968, 227.

194. Fortuna
- 'Fortunae / sacrum' (Pastor Muñoz 1976:506).
- Location = Astorga
- Dedicator = Unknown
- References = Pastor Muñoz 1976:506; Tranoy 1981:322; Mañanez Perez 1982:no.3; CIL II 5664; ILER 442.

195. Fortuna
- 'L. Versenus / Aper Praef/ Alae opere / balinei . sub se / incohato et / consumma/to Fortunae / l.v.s' (AE 1937, 166). The inscription is related to bath establishments at the camp (Tranoy 1981:321)
- Location = Petavonium, Rosinos de Vidriales (Zamora)
- Dedicator = L. Versenus Aper
- References = AE 1937, 166; Tranoy 1981:321.

196. Fortuna Balneari (Of the Baths)
- 'Fortunae / Balneari / T. Pompeius Pe/regrinianus / pro salute / sua et suorum / dicauit' (ERA, no.6).
- Location = Pumarín, (Gijón)
- Dedicator = Titus Pompeius Peregrinianus
- References = ERA, no. 6; Pastor Muñoz 1976:506; Tranoy 1981:320-1; CIL II 2701; ILER 450.

197. Fortuna Bona Redux
- 'Fortunae / Bonae Reduci / Ul(pius) Maximus / proc(urator) Aug(usti) / cum uxore / et filio' (Pastor Muñoz 1976:505). In Mañanez Perez, no.5: 'P(ublius) Ul(pius) Maximus.'
- Location = Astorga
- Dedicator(s) = Ulpius Maximus (the Procurator) with his wife and son.
- References = Pastor Muñoz 1976:505; Tranoy 1981:321; Mañanez Perez 1982:no.5; AE 1968, 223.

198. Fortuna Redux Sancta
- 'Fortuna Reduci Sanctae / G. Otacilius Octavius / Saturninusque proc(urator) / Aug(usti) dicauit cum filia et nepote (Pastor Muñoz 1976:505). Also, line 3 as: 'Saturninus V(ir) E(gregivs)' in Mañanez Perez, no.6.
- Location = Astorga
- Dedicator = G. Otacilius Octavius Saturninus (Procurator) and his daughter and granddaughter.
- References = Pastor Muñoz 1976:505; Tranoy 1981:321; Mañanez Perez 1982:no.6; AE 1968, 234.

199. Genius
- 'Genio [---] / ------' (AE 1999, 919b).
- Location = Boñar, León.
- Dedicator = Unsure
- References = AE 1999, 919b; CIL II 5726.

200. Genius (of Conventus Asturicenses)
- 'Genio / Convent(us) / Asturicensis' (Mañanez Perez 1982:no.7)
- Location = Astorga
- Dedicator = Unknown
- References = Mañanez Perez 1982:no.7; CIL II 4072; Pastor Muñoz 1976:506-7.

201. Genius (of the Legio VII Gemina)
- 'Genio / leg(ionis) VII/ (piae felicis) L. Attius / Marco leg(atus) Aug(usti)' (Pastor Muñoz 1976:507).
- Location = León
- Dedicator = The legatus Augusti, Lucius Attius Macro.
- References = Pastor Muñoz 1976:507; Tranoy 1981:322; Quintana Prieto 1969:62; CIL II 5083; ILER 554.

202. Genius (of the Legio VII Gemina)
- 'Genio (leg(ionis)) VII G(eminae) f(elicis) d(ecianae) T(raianae) / Cl(audius) Pom/peianus (s)t(ipendiodum) XIV g(ratus) u(obis)' (Pastor Muñoz 1976:507). García y Bellido has a similar translation (1971:148-9) but Tranoy translates this differently with the dedicator being Tiberius Claudius Pompeianus and the vow being 'ex iussu Genii' (1981:322).
- Location = León
- Dedicator = Claudius Pompeianus (Pastor Muñoz 1976:507) or the tribune Tiberius Claudius Pompeianus (Tranoy 1981:322).
- References = Pastor Muñoz 1976:507; Tranoy 1981:322; AE 1974, 411; García y Bellido 1971:148-9.

203. Hercules
- 'Herculi sacr(um) / M. Sallius L. F. Arn(ensis) / Honoratus do/mo choba ex pr/ovincia Maur(e)tania Caes(ariense) pra(e)/f(ectus) eq(uitum) A(lae) II F(laviae) H(ispanorum) c(ivium) R(omanorum) / votorum compo/s templa Alcidi / Deo a fundame/ntis exstruxit' (Pastor Muñoz 1976:510).
- Loc = Petavonium, Rosinos de Vidriales (Zamora), 30km NW of Benavente (Pastor Muñoz 1976:510).
- Dedicator = M. Sellius Honoratus of the Ala II Flavia, (originally from Mauritania)
- References = Tranoy 1981:311; Pastor Muñoz 1976:510; Mañanez Perez 1982:no.109; AE 1963, 16; ILER 194.

204. Juno Regina and the health of the Emperor
- 'Iunoni Reginae / pro salute ac Imp(erii) diurnitate (Imp.) M. Aurelli Antonini / pii fel. Aug. et Iulia(e) piae fel. Aug. matri(s) / Antonini Aug. Ca(s)trorum Senatus / ac Patriae / C. Iul. Cerealis co(n)s(uli) / Anton(i)nianae post

divission(em) provinc(iae) primus ab eo m(issus)/' (Pastor Muñoz 1976:511).
- Location = León
- Dedicator = C. Julius Cerealis (Consul who becomes a legatus Augusti pro praetore of the Provincia Hispania Nova Citerior Antoniana – Pastor Muñoz 1976:510-11).
- References = Pastor Muñoz 1976:510-11; HE 1989, no.390; CIL II 2661.

205. Jupiter
- 'Iovi / C(enturia – with inverted C) Que/ledi/ni' (Mañanez Perez 1982:no.110).
- Location = San Andrés de Montejos (León).
- Dedicators = The centuria or gentilitas 'Queledini.'
- References = Mañanez Perez 1982:no.110; Pastor Muñoz 1976:496; Tranoy 1981:316; ILER 84.

206. Jupiter
- 'Iovis / n(ostri?)' (AE 1990, 552).
- Location = Astorga
- Dedicator = Unsure
- References = AE 1990, 552.

207. Jupiter
- 'Iuliano II et Crispino cos Prid[-]idus Februarias Aemilias Cilimedus / pro salute sua e suorum die Iovis' (AE 1962, 397).
- Location = Villadecanos
- Dedicator = Aemilius Cilimedus
- References = AE 1962, 397; Tranoy 1981:317.

208. I.O.M.
- 'Iovi Opt/ et Max A/pp Claud / f' (CIL II 2400).
- Location = Travanca
- Dedicator = Appius Claudius
- References = CIL II 2400; ILER 89; Tranoy 1981:317.

209. • Jupiter Optimus Maximus
- Jupiter Optimus Maximus (Tranoy 1981:317)
- Location = Trives (/Santa Maria de Trives).
- Dedicators = Severus, son of Flavinus

- References = Tranoy 1981:317; Ramirez 1981:243.

210. Jupiter Optimus Maximus
- 'Iovi Optimo et / Maximo Potentis/simo Civitas Tra/nensis P' (CIL II 2399).
- Location = S. Mamede (Moncorvo)
- Dedicators = Unsure (Civitas Tranensis)
- References = CIL II 2399; Tranoy 1981:317.

211. Jupiter Optimus Maximus
- 'I.O.M. / T. I. L. / et pp / ex vo/to' (EE IX, 276).
- Location = Babe
- Dedicators = Unknown
- References = EE IX, 276; Tranoy 1981:318.

212. • Jupiter Optimus Maximus
- Jupiter Optimus Maximus (Tranoy 1981:318)
- Location = Carviçães
- Dedicators = Unknown (Tranoy 1981:318).
- References = Tranoy 1981:318.

213. Jupiter Optimus Maximus
- 'I(ovi) O(ptimo) M(aximo)' (Mañanez Perez 1982:no.8).
- Location = Astorga
- Dedicators = Unknown
- References = Mañanez Perez 1982:no.8; Tranoy 1981:318; Quintana Prieto, 88, no.134.

214. Jupiter Optimus Maximus
- 'Iovi Optimo / Maximo' (ERA, no.2).
- Location = Castiello, Gijón.
- Dedicator = Unknown
- References = Pastor Muñoz 1976:495; Tranoy 1981:318; CIL II 2702; ERA, no.2; ILER 1.

215. Jupiter Optimus Maximus
- 'Iovi Op[ti]/mo Max[si]/mo sacr[u]/m' (ERA, no.4).
- Location = Rellón de Merás (Luarca).
- Dedicator = Unknown
- References = Pastor Muñoz 1976:495; Tranoy 1981:318; CIL II 2693; ERA, no.4, pp.28-9.

216. Jupiter Optimus Maximus
- 'Iovi Optimo / et Maxsumo / sacrum . Arro/nidaeci et Col/iacini pro sal/ute sibi et suis posuerunt' (ERA, no.1).
- Location = San Vicente de Serrapio, Concejo de Aller (Oviedo).
- Dedicator = The indigenous Gentilitates of the Arronidaeci and Coliacini (Pastor Muñoz 1976:495).
- References = ERA, no.1; Pastor Muñoz 1976:495; Tranoy 1981:316; CIL II 2697; ILER 15.

217. Jupiter Optimus Maximus
- 'I(ovi) O(ptimo) M(aximo) M(arcus) Ian(uarius) pro s(alute) / F(abi) Muci Calist/iani v(otum) l(ibenter) s(oluit)' (Pastor Muñoz 1976:496).
- Location = Crémenes (León)
- Dedicator = M. Ianuarius (in favour of F. Mucius Calistianus).
- References = Pastor Muñoz 1976:496; ILER 20.

218. Jupiter Optimus Maximus
- 'I(ovi) O(ptimo) M(aximo) Cattulinus vir consu/laris praeses prov(inciae) Call(aeciae) pro salute sua suorumque omnium posuit' (Pastor Muñoz 1976:497). Tranoy has the dedicator as 'Aco Catullinus' (Tranoy 1981:316).
- Location = Astorga
- Dedicator = Cattulinus (Pastor Muñoz 1976:497).
- References = Pastor Muñoz 1976:497; Tranoy 1981:316; CIL II 2635; Mañanez Perez 1982:no.9; ILER 22.

219. Jupiter Optimus Maximus and the health of the Emperors
- 'I.O.M./ [p]ro salute . M . Aureli An/[i]onini. et. L. Aureli. Veri / [a]ugustor . ob . natale . aqu[i]/lae . vexillatio leg . VII . Gf / sub. cura . Licini . patern[i] / 7 . leg. eiusd . et . hermetis / Augustor . lib . proc . et . Lu/creti . paterni . dec . coh . I . Celt . et . Fabi . Marcian[i] / B F proc . Augustor . et / Iuli . Iuliani sign . Leg / euisd . III id Iunias / Lealiano et Pastore [cos]' (Mañanez Perez 1982:no.114).
- Location = Villalis
- Dedicator = Legio VII.
- References = Mañanez Perez 1982:no.114; Tranoy 1981:316; Pastor Muñoz 1976:496; CIL II 2552; ILER 24.

220. Jupiter Optimus Maximus and the health of the Emperors
- 'I.O.M. / pro salutem . Aureli Antonini / et . L. Aureli . Veri Augustorum / ob natale signor . vexillatio / coh I Celtib sub cura Zoili / Augustor . lib proc . et . Vel . Flav[i]

/ 7 . coh I Gall . et Aeli Falvi B . F proc / Augustor . et Lucreti . Mater/ni . Imag . leg . VII G F . et Iuli Se/ duli Tesserari . c . t . c . posita / idib octobrib Imp . L . Aure/lio Vero III et Quadrato cos' (Mañanez Perez 1982:no.116).
- Location = Villalis
- Dedicator = Cohort I Celt.
- References = Mañanez Perez 1982:no.116; Tranoy 1981:316; Pastor Muñoz 1976:496; CIL II 2553; ILER 25.

221. Jupiter Optimus Maximus and the health of the Emperors
- 'I.O.M. / pro sal M A(ur) / Ant[onini Aug] / ob natale aqui/lae vexilla[tio] / leg VII G f sub cu/ra Aur Euthych[is] / Aug lib proc . et . [Val] / Semproniani [dec] / alae II Flaviae IIII I[d] / Iun Marullio et Aeliano / cos' (Mañanez Perez 1982: no.118).
- Location = Villalis
- Dedicator = Legio VII.
- References = Mañanez Perez 1982:no.118; Tranoy 1981:316; Pastor Muñoz 1976:496; CIL II 2554; Vigil 1961:107; ILER 26.

222. Jupiter Optimus Maximus and the health of the Emperors
- 'I(ovi) O(ptimo) M(aximo) / pro salute M. Aurelli / Antonini et L. Aurelli Veri / Augustorum / ob natale[m] . . . . . leg(ionis) VII Ge[minae] / milites coh(ortis) I Gall[a]eco[rum] / sub cura . . . emet . . . Aug(ustorum) / lib(erti) [proc(uratoris)] et L[u]cret(i) Patern[I dec(urionis)] / coh(ortis) [I Celtiberorum] et Ful[vi. . . . . .] . . .' (CIL II 2555).
- Location = Villalis
- Dedicator = Legio VII.
- References = Tranoy 1981:316; Pastor Muñoz 1976:496; CIL II 2555.

223. Jupiter Optimus Maximus and the health of the Emperors
- 'I.O.M. / [pro salute M. Aureli] / Anton[ini et L. Aureli] / Ver A V [Gustor o]B [Natale] / Aprun(color) Mil(ites) / coh I Gall sub cura(zo) / [i]li Augustor lib pro[c] / [et] Val Flavi 7 coh ei(us) / [de]m . et Val Valentis [b f] / [pr]oc August[or] et Iu[li] / [Iu]iani signif leg VII G [f] / [X .K] Maias Pud … [cos]' (Mañanez Perez 1982:no.115).
- Location = Villalis
- Dedicator = Cohort I Gal.
- References = Mañanez Perez 1982:no.115; Tranoy 1981:316; Pastor Muñoz 1976:496; CIL II 2556; ILER 27.

224. Jupiter Optimus Maximus and the health of the Emperors
- 'I.O.M.s / pro. salute. Imp/ Caes. M. Aur. Anto/nini. Aug. ob nata[le] / Aprunculorum / milites. coh. I. Gal / sub cura M Senti / Bucconis ..) coh. eiusd / et. Val. Semproniani(i) / Beneficiari proc. Aug/ X. K. AAI. Pisone et Iulino. cos' (Mañanez Perez 1982:no.117).
- Location = Villalis
- Dedicator = Cohort I Gal.
- References = Mañanez Perez 1982:no.117; Tranoy 1981:316; Pastor Muñoz 1976:496; ILER 28.

225. Jupiter Optimus Maximus and the health of the Emperors
- '[I.O.M. / pro salute M. Aure/li Commodi An]/tonini Pii. Fel Au[g] / Ger. Max. trib. pot / imp XV. cos VI. ob. N[a]/tale. Aprungulorum / milit. sub. cu[ra] / Aurelii. Firmi. Aug. lib / met. et. Valeri Marcell[i] / dec. Al II Fl. X. K. Ma[i/a]s Opilio Pedone et / [B]radua. Mauri[co cos].' (Mañanez Perez 1982:no.119).
- Location = Villalis
- Dedicator = Cohort I Gal.
- References = Mañanez Perez 1982:no.119; Tranoy 1981:316; Pastor Muñoz 1976:496; Vigil 1961:107-8; ILER 29.

226. Jupiter Optimus Maximus and the health of the Emperors
- 'I.O.M. / pro salute. M. Aurel. Antonini' (Mañanez Perez 1982:no.120).
- Location = Villalis
- Dedicator = Unsure (Fragment).
- References = Mañanez Perez 1982:no.120; Tranoy 1981:316; Pastor Muñoz 1976:496; ILER 21; AE 1965, 66.

227. Jupiter Optimus Maximus and the health of the Emperor
- 'I(ovi) O(ptimo) M(aximo) / pro salute / T(iti) Ael(ii) Hadrian(i) / Anton(ini) Aug(usti) Pii / Vex(illatio) Leg(ionis) VII G(eminae) F(elicis) / sub cur(a) Ivl(ii) Mar/ci C(enturionis) eiusd(em) et Val(erii) / Victoris dec(urionis) ob / diem nata(lis) Aquilae / v(otum) s(olvit) l(ibens) m(erito)' (Mañanez Perez 1982:no.112).
- Location = Luyego
- Dedicator = Legio VII
- References = Mañanez Perez 1982:no.112; Tranoy 1981:316; Pastor Muñoz 1976:496; García y Bellido 1966:24-26.

228. Jupiter Optimus Maximus and the health of the Emperor
- 'I(ovi) O(ptimo) M(aximo) / pro salute L(ucii) Aurel(ii) / Commodi Aug(usti) ob / natale(m) Aquil(a)e Leg(ionis) / VII G(eminae) F(elicis) sub cura M(arci) Avr(elii) Evtichetis A(ugusti?) / Proc(uratoris) et Coh(ortis) I Galli(cae) et Aviti Patern[i] / Aug(usto) / et Buro Co(n)s(ulibus)' (Mañanez Perez 1982:no.113).
- Location = Luyego
- Dedicator = Legio VII Gemina
- References = Mañanez Perez 1982:no.113; Tranoy 1981:316; Pastor Muñoz 1976:496; García y Bellido 1966:26-7.

229. Jupiter Optimus Maximus Capitolinus
- 'Iovi Op(timo) M(aximo) Cap(itolino) / Gaius Oc/tavi(us) ex (voto) posuit' (Pastor Muñoz 1976:497). Interestingly this altar is engraved with the head of a bull (Pastor Muñoz 1976:497).
- Location = Torre de Santa Marina (León) (in the region of Bierzo).
- Dedicator = Gaius Octavius
- References = Pastor Muñoz 1976:496-7; Tranoy 1981:317; ILER 144.

230. Jupiter Optimus Maximus Custodus, Juno Regina, Minerva Sancta and all the Gods
- 'I(ovi) O(ptimo) M(aximo) / Custodi / Iunoni Reginae / Minervae Sanctae / ceterisque Dis / Deabusque / Inmortalibus / Iulius Silvanus / Melanio proc(urator) Augg(ustorum) / provinc(iae) Hisp(aniae) Citer(ioris) / dicauit' (Pastor Muñoz 1976:498).
- Location = Astorga
- Dedicator = C. Iulius Silvanus Melanio (Procurator).
- References = Tranoy 1981:311; Pastor Muñoz 1976:498; Mañanez Perez 1982:no.11; AE 1968, 229.

231. Jupiter Optimus Maximus Depulsor or Dolichenus
- 'I(ovi) O(ptimo) M(aximo) D(epulsori) (or D(olichenus)) / Domitius Peregrinus / (Septimae) / ge(minae) p(iae) f(elicis) / v(otum) s(oluit) l(ibens) m(erito)' (AE 1974, 393).

- Location = Saldanha
- Dedicator = Domitius Peregrinus
- References = AE 1974, 393; AE 1987, 606; Tranoy 1981:317.

232. Jupiter Optimus Maximus, Juno Regina and Minerva Victrix and the health of the Emperor
- 'Iovi Optimo Maximo / Iunoni Reginae / Minervae Victrici / P(ublius) Ael(ius) Hilarianus / proc(urator) Aug(usti) cum liberis / pro salute ...Aug(usti) Pii Fel(ilicis)' (Pastor Muňoz 1976:498). Maňanez Perez 1982:no.10, has: line 4 = '/P(ublius) Ael(ius), P(ubli) F(ilius) Hilarianus/' and line 6 = '/pro salute [imp(eratoris) Caes(aris) Aug(usti)/.'
- Location = Astorga
- Dedicator = Publius Aelius Hilarianus (Procurator).
- References = Pastor Muňoz 1976:498; Maňanez Peres 1982:no.10; Tranoy 1981:316; AE 1968, 228.

233. Jupiter Optimus Maximus, Sol Invictus, Liber Patri, Genius Praetorii
- 'I(ovi) O(ptimo) M(aximo) Soli Invicto Libero / Patri Genio Praetor(ii) / Q(uintus) Mamil(ius) Capitolinus / Iurid(icus) per flaminiam / et umbriam et picenum / leg(atus) Aug(usti) per Asturiam et / Callaeciam dux leg(ionis) VII G(eminae) P(iae) Fe(licis) / praef(ectus) Aer(arii) Sat(urni) pro salute / sua et suorum' (Pastor Muňoz 1976:497-8).
- Location = Astorga
- Dedicator = Q. Mamilius Capitolinus (Juridical Legate of the Severan era)
- References = Tranoy 1981:311; Pastor Muňoz 1976:497-8; Maňanez Perez 1982:no.12; CIL II 2634; ILER 151.

234. Jupiter, Serapis and Iao (Bacchus/Dionysius)
- 'ΕΙCΖΣYC / CΣPAΠIC / IAW' (Maňanez Perez 1982:no.111).
- Location = The town of Quintanilla de Somoza, around 15kms from Astorga.
- Dedicator = Unknown
- References = Maňanez Perez 1982:no.111; Tranoy 1981:336; CIL II 5665.

235. Lares Viales
- 'Q(uintus) P(ublicus?) / Laribus / Vialibus/ ex voto' (ERA, no.5).
- Location = Santiaňes de Tuňa (Tineo)
- Dedicator = Quintus Publicus (?)
- References = ERA, no.5; Pastor Muňoz 1976:511-12; CIL II 5734.

236. Lares Viales
- 'Sem(pronius) Cas(sius) / Laribus / Vialibus / ex voto / sacrum' (HE 1989, no.78).
- Location = Found in 1983 at Tuňa (Tineo).
- Dedicator = Sempronius Cassius
- References = HE 1989, no.78.

237. Liber Pater
- 'Libero Patri / G(aius) Vet(t)ius / Felicio' (IRG IV, 72).
- Location = San Pedro de Montes, valley of Valdeorras (Orense).
- Dedicator = G. Vettius Felicio
- References = Tranoy 1981:311; CIL II 2611; IRG IV 72; Pastor Muňoz 1976:512; ILER 213.

238. Liber Pater Conservator
- 'Libero / Patri / Conser(v)a/(tori) ... ...ius/'(Pastor Muňoz 1976:513). This is a very fragmentary altar with Dionysiac decoration (Tranoy 1981:311).
- Location = León
- Dedicator = Unknown
- References = Tranoy 1981:311; Pastor Muňoz 1976:513.

239. Mars
- '/Marte /' (Pastor Muňoz 1976:516). The rest of the text is incomprehensible; it is an engraving on a plaque made of terracotta (Tranoy 1981:314).
- Location = The site of the village of Navatejera, on the Torío river, 3 km north of León.
- Dedicator = Unknown.
- References = Tranoy 1981:314; Pastor Muňoz 1976:516.

240. Mars Gradivus
- 'Marti / Gradivo / L. Didius Ma/rinus proc(urator) Aug(ustorum) ex voto / fecit' (Pastor Muňoz 1976:518). The epithet 'Gradivus' is not taken to be indigenous by Tranoy, Pastor Muňoz, and Maňanez Perez, who see the epithet as referring to Mars as a protector of the harvest. Also ancient authors mention a temple of Mars Gravidus in Rome – RE VII, 1688; SER. Aen. I.272 (Pastor Muňoz 1976:518). Blázquez (1962:191) and Quintana Prieto (1969:64-5) refer to this deity as indigenous.
- Location = Astorga
- Dedicator = L. Didius Marinus
- References = Tranoy 1981:314; Pastor Muňoz 1976:518; Blázquez 1962:.121; Quintana Prieto p.64-5; Maňanez Perez 1982:no.14.

241. Mercury
- 'Mercurio / [sac]rum /Fel(ix) ex v(oto) p(osuit)' (Pastor Muňoz 1976:519).
- Location = (Villar de los Barrios) León
- Dedicator = Felix
- References = Tranoy 1981:315; Pastor Muňoz 1976:519; CIL II 5706; ILER 259.

242. Mercury
- 'Mercurio / [sac]rum / Flaccus Aelianu(s) / proc(urator) Aug(u)sto / v(otum) s(oluit) l(ibens) m(erito)' (Pastor Muňoz 1976:519).
- Location = León
- Dedicator = Flaccus Aelianus (procurator).
- References = Pastor Muňoz 1976:519; CIL II 5678; ILER 261; Tranoy 1981:315.

243. Minerva
- 'Flavin/us Min/ervae v(otum) s(oluit) l(ibens) m(erito)' (Pastor Muňoz 1976:519).
- Location = León
- Dedicator = Flavinus
- References = Pastor Muňoz 1976:519.

244. Minerva, Juno Victrix and the health of the Emperor
- 'Minervae et I[unoni Victrici ac] / Patriae Conserv(atrici) [pro sal(ute) Iuliae Aug(ustae)] Matris / imp(eratoris) Caes(aris) M(arci) Au[r(elii) Antonini et] P(ublii) Septim(i) / Severi [Getae] / Pi(a)e Fel(ius) A[ug(ustae) et Matris Senat]us et cast/ror[um et Patriae --- S]acrum' (HE 1989, no.391). Also, in an older lecture as: 'Minervae et (Magnae Deum) Matri i (Deae) / Patriae Conserv(atricibus)s e n. imp / Caes. M. Aur. (Cari Cur.)

ante Castino u(iro) / c(on)s dedicatum e(x) v(oto)' (Pastor Muňoz 1976:519-20).
- Location = León
- Dedicator = Castinus
- References = Pastor Muňoz 1976:519-20; HE 1989, no.391.

245. Mithras
- 'Ponit Inv/icto Deo / Austo [which is short for Augustus] . Po/nit lebien/s Fronto / aram
  Invi/cto Deo Au/sto . Pleveiu/s [= Fronto levens?] point pr(a)e/sedente pa/tron patra/tum Leone / M(ithrae)' (ERA, no.7).
- Location = La Isla (Colunga)
- Dedicator = Fronto, Oviedo
- References = ERA, no.7; Tranoy 1981:335; CIL II 2705 & 5728.

246. Nemesis
- 'Nemesi / vo(tum) sol(uit) / Reburrus' (AE 1995, 856).
- Location = Petauonium (Rosinos de Vidriales), camp of Alae II Flavienne.
- Dedicator = Reburrus
- References = AE 1995, 856.

247. Nymphs
- 'Nymphis / T. Pomponius / Proculus / Vitrasius / Pollio co(n)s Pontif(ex) proco(n)s. / Asiae leg(atus) Aug(usti) / Provinciar(um) / Moesia Inf(erioris) et / Hisp(aniae) Cit(erioris) et Faustina (filia) eius' (Pastor Muňoz 1976:521).
- Location = Leon
- Dedicator = T. Pomponius Proculus Vitrasius Pollio, and his daughter (wife) Faustina
- References = Pastor Muňoz 1976:521; Tranoy 1981:324; CIL II 5679; ILER 605.

248. Nymphs
- 'Nymphis / sacr(um) / A. Cornelius / Anteros im/agnifer le(gionis)VII G(emina) F(elicis) / cum vexillati/one v(otum) s(oluit) l(ibens) m(erito)' (Pastor Muňoz 1976:521). Tranoy (1981:324) has the dedicator as: 'Q. Valerius Anteros.'
- Location = Leon
- Dedicator = A. Cornelius Anteros and his auxiliary
- References = Pastor Muňoz 1976:521; Tranoy 1981:324.

249. Nymphs (Fontis Amecni/Ameui)
- 'Nymphis / Fontis Ameu/cn(i) / L. Terentius / L.F. Homollus / Iunior leg(atus) leg(ionis) VII G(eminae) F(elicis) l(ibens) v(otum) m(erito) s(oluit)' (Pastor Muňoz 1976:522). Tranoy's reading has 'Fontis Ameui,' and the dedicator as 'Cn. L. Terentius Homullus'(1981:324).
- Location = León
- Dedicator = L. Terentius Homullus Junior legate of the Legio VII Gemina.
- References = Tranoy 1981:324; Pastor Muňoz 1976:522; CIL II 5084; Blázquez 1962:169; ILER 695.

250. Serapis and Isis
- 'Invicto Deo / Seapidi et / Isidi / Cl(audius) Zenobius proc(urator) Aug(usti)' (Maňanez Perez 1982:no.15).
- Location = Astorga (Found with Maňanez Perez's nos.2,4,5,6,11,12, and 16).
- Dedicator = The procurator, Claudius Zenobius
- References = Maňanez Perez 1982:no.15; AE 1968, 232.

* See also the dedication to Serapis Sanctus, Isis Mirionima, Core Invicta, Apollo Grannus, Mars Sagatus (No.37, Cat.III).

251. Silvanus
- 'Silvano / Apilici f(ilio) / S(ilvanus) d(edicauit)' (AE 1987, 585).
- Location = Duas Igrejas, Miranda.
- Dedicator = Silvanus son of Apilicus
- References = AE 1987, 585; CIL II 5660.

Uncertain Readings from the Conventus Asturum

252. (Genius) Populi(?) or Porolus?
- 'M(arcus) Aemili/[u]S Lepid[i]/nus Pop/[u]lo v(otum) s(oluit) l(ibens) m(erito)' (IRG IV, 99). In AE 1987, 562d as: ' M(arcus) Aemili/[u]s Lepidi/nus Por[o]/lo v(otum) s(oluit) l(ibens) m(erito).'
- Location = Vilamartín de Valdeorras, Orense
- Dedicator = M. Aemilius Lepidinus
- References = IRG IV, 99; AE 1987, 562d.

253. Jupiter Optimus Maximus
- '[I(ovi) O(ptimo)?] M(aximo) /...' (AE 1991, 1043).
- Location = Destriana
- Dedicator = Unsure
- References = AE 1991, 1043.

Location Unsure in the North-West

254. Jupiter Optimus Maximus
- '[I]ovi Op/timo Ma/xumo, Cornelius Vi/talis votu/m promis/it' (AE 1974, 314).
- Location = Imprecise location in north-west Iberia (perhaps Bragance?).
- Dedicator = Cornelius Vitalis
- References = Tranoy 1981:317; AE 1973, 314.

255. Mars
- 'Ma(rt)i Patri / Tib . Iunius / Tib fil . Quir / Quadratus / domo Roma / praef. equit. Al/ II. Fl. Hisp / C. R .....'(CIL II 2600).
- Location = Imprecise location in north-west Iberia.
- Dedicator = Tib. Iunius Quir Quadratus (A soldier originally from Rome).
- References = Tranoy 1981:314; Ramirez 1981:244; CIL II 2600; ILER 221.

256. Tutela
- 'Tutelae / L(ucius) Antonius / Avitus cum / filis et Zozima l(iberta) / ex voto' (Arias Vilas, Le Roux & Tranoy 1979:no.73.).
- Location = Imprecise location in north-west Iberia (perhaps Lucensis?).
- Dedicator = The freedman Lucius Antonius Avitus, with his son and Zozima
- References = Arias Vilas, Le Roux & Tranoy 1979:no.73; Tranoy 1981:322; CIL II 2538; ILER 483.

Catalogue III
Classical Deities with Indigenous Epithets
Conventus Bracaraugustanus

1. Genius Laquinesis
   - 'votum lb. s. m / Genio L/aquini/esi Flav. Flavini fu.llo // Ge(nio) La(quin.)' (ILER 658).
   - Location = S. Miguel das Caldas de Vizuela (Guimarâes)
   - Dedicator = Flavus, son of Flavinus (a fuller)
   - References = Tranoy 1981:302; CIL II 2405; Blázquez 1962:135; Encarnaçâo 1975:191-192; ILER 658.

2. Genius Macellus
   - 'Genio / Macelli / Flavius / Urbicio / ex voto / posuit / sacrum' (CIL II 2413).
   - Location = Braga (the village of Macellus?).
   - Dedicator = Flavius Urbicio
   - References = Tranoy 1981:322; CIL II 2413; ILER 547.

3. Genius Tiauranceaicus
   - 'Camala Ar/qui f(ilia) Tal/abrigen/sis Genio T/iauranceai/co v(otum) s(oluit) l(ibens) m(erito)' (Blázquez 1962:135).
   - Location = Estorâos (Ponte de Lima).
   - Dedicator = Camala, daughter of Arquius
   - References = Tranoy 1981:302; Blázquez 1962:135; Encarnaçâo 1975:192-5; ILER 659.

4. Genius Tongobricensium
   - '[G]enio / [L or T]on[g]obr/[i]censium [Fl]avius v.s.a.l.m.' (CIL II 5564).
   - Location = Friexo (Marco de Canveses).
   - Dedicator = Flavius
   - References = Tranoy 1981:302; CIL II 5564; Blázquez 1962:135-136; Encarnaçâo 1975:195-7; ILER 660.

5. Hermes Devoris
   - 'Ermaei De/vori ob ev/entum bo/num gladi/atori m[u]neris Cexaec/us Fuscu/s x ex / voto'(Blázquez 1962:134).
   - Location = Outeiro Seco, Chaves.
   - Dedicator = Cexaecus Fuscus (who set up this altar for the success obtained by a munus of Gladiators).
   - References = Blázquez 1962:133-5; Tranoy 1981:302; CIL II 2473; ILER 661 and 5992.

6. Lar Beiraidegus
   - 'Lucr[etiu]/s Caturon[i]/s f(ilius) Lari B/eiradi[e]/go ex vot(o) / pos(uit) ar(a) sac(rauit or –ram)' (AE 1983, 560).
   - Location = Church of Sta. Maria de Arnoso, Vila Nova de Famalicâo (Braga).
   - Dedicator = Lucretius, son of Caturo
   - References = AE 1983, 560; Tranoy 1981:303-4.

7. Lar Cariecus
   - 'Aur(elius) Fla/vus Lar/i Cari[e]co / votum / [libe]ns / [so]luit' (AE 1983:561). Though this may also be read as 'Mar[t]I Cari[e]co' (AE 1983:561).
   - Loc = Chapel of Sta. Eulalia, Refojos de Lima (Ponte de Lima).
   - Dedicator = Aurelius Flavus
   - References = AE 1983, 561; Tranoy 1981:303-4.

8. Lar Circeiebaecus Proeneiaecus
   - 'Lari / Circeiebaeco Proeneiaeco L(ucius) Campanius Macer v(otum) s(oluit) l(ibens) m(erito)' (Rodríguez Colmenero 1977:309).
   - Location = Santa Marta de Moreiras
   - Dedicator = L. Campanius Macer
   - References = Tranoy 1981:303-4; Ramirez 1981:247; Rodríguez Colmenero 1977:309; AE 1974, 408.

9. Lar Pemaneiecus
   - 'Lar Pem/aneieco / exs vis (?)' (AE 1974:409). Rodríguez Colmenero has 'Pemaneiego' (1977:310).
   - Location = San Pedro de Readegos
   - Dedicator = Unknown
   - References = Tranoy 1981:303; Ramirez 1981:247; AE 1974, 409; Rodríguez Colemenero 1977:310.

10. Lar Sefius ?
    - 'Larisefi/o Com/es pro sa/lute sua/ et suoru(m)' (Blázquez 1962:133).
    - Location = Adaúfe, Concejo de Braga
    - Dedicator = Comes ?
    - References = Blázquez 1962:133; Tranoy 1981:303-4; Encarnaçâo 1975:220-221; ILER 861.

11. Lares Burici
    - '[L]aribus / [B]uricis / [V]otum / [S]oluit / Bloena' (AE 1973:320).
    - Location = Carrazedo (S. Martinho, Amares).
    - Dedicator = Bloena
    - References = Tranoy 1981:303; Alarcâo 1988, Vol.II:1/202; AE 1973, 320.

12. Lares Cerenaeci
    - 'Laribus / Cerena/ecis Nig/er Proc/uli f v l s' (CIL II 2384).
    - Location = S. Salvador de Tuias (Marco de Canaveses).
    - Dedicator = Niger, son of Proculus
    - References = Tranoy 1981:303; Ramirez 1981:247; CIL II 2384; Blázquez 1962:131; Encarnaçâo 1975:211-212; ILER 674.

13. Lares Cusicfllenses
    - 'Laribus Cusicflensibus Q Nivius Placidi f(ilius) envins? / v(otum) s(oluit) l(ibens) m(erito)' (Rodríguez Colemenero 1977:310). ILER 678 has: 'Laribus Cu/sicelensibus.'
    - Location = Couto de Algeriz (Chaves)
    - Dedicator = Q. Nivius, son of Placidus
    - References = Rodríguez Colmenero 1977:310; Tranoy 1981:303; Ramirez 1981:247; CIL II 2469; Blázquez 1962:131; Encarnaçâo 1975:212-213; ILER 678.

14. Lares Erredici
    - 'Laribus Erredi(cis) S(ulpicius) Rufus ex voto' (Rodríguez Colmenero 1977:310).
    - Location = S. Pedro de Agostem (Chaves)
    - Dedicator = S. Rufus
    - References = Rodríguez Colmenero 1977:310; Tranoy 1981:303; Ramirez 1981:247; CIL II 2470; Blázquez 1962:132; ILER 675.

15. Lares Findeneici
    - 'Albinus Balesini Lari(b)us Findeneicis libens posui(t)' (Rodríguez Colmenero 1977:310).
    - Location = Chaves
    - Dedicator = Albinus, son of Balesinus
    - References = Rodríguez Colmenero 1977:310; Tranoy 1981:303; CIL II 2471; Blázquez 1962:132; Encarnaçâo 1975:214-216; Leite de Vasconcelos 1905:181-2; ILER

676.

16. Lares Gegeiqis
- 'Mauxumus (sic) / Trupeisi f(ilius) / Rufin(us) L(airbus) / Gegeiqis / v(otum) s(oluit) l(ibens) m(erito)' (AE 1987, 572c).
- Location = Arcossó, Chaves.
- Dedicator = Mauxumus Rufinus son of Trupeisus
- References = AE 1987, 572c.

17. Lares Gumeinus
- 'M(arcus) Licinius / Veleiensis / Laribus / Gumeinu / v(otum) s(oluit) l(ibens) m(erito), (AE 1981, 530). Tranoy has: 'Lares Cumelani' (1981:303).
- Location = Vilanova de Infantes, Celanova.
- Dedicator = M. Licinius of the Veleienses(?)
- References = AE 1981, 530; Tranoy 1981:303.

18. Lares Ormonufis
- 'Larib(us) Orm/onufis / S(ulpicius) Coraec(us) / v(otum) l(ibens) s(oluit) m(erito)' (AE 1987, 562k).
- Location = Pitôes de Junias, Montalegre.
- Dedicator = Sulpicius Coraecus
- References = AE 1987, 562k.

19. Lares Taremucenbaeci Ceceaeci (or Oeceaecis)
- 'Laribus Taremucenbaecis Ceceacis Aelius Flavus v(otum) s(oluit) l(ibens) m(erito)' (Rodríguez Colmenero 1977:310). Alarcão and Ramirez have : 'Laribus Tarmucenbaecis Oeceaecis' (Alarcão 1988, Vol.II:1/118; Ramirez 1981:247).
- Location = Granjinha, Vale de Anta (Chaves)
- Dedicator = P. Aelius Flavius
- References = Rodríguez Colmenero 1977:310; Tranoy 1981:303; CIL II 2472; Blázquez 1962:130-1; Encarnação 1975:217-18; ILER 679; AE, 1973, 312.

20. Mars Cairiogiegus
- 'Marti Cai/riogiego / L(ucius) Hispani/us Fronto / ex voto / sacrum' (CIRG II, no.115). 'Mars Capriociegus' in Tranoy 1981:304 and 'Mars Capriociecus' in ILER 684. Also many have taken the surname as 'Cariociegus' = CIL II 5612; Blázquez 1962:115; IRG III,16 (Cariociecus).
- Location = The village of Tuy, on the bank of the Miño.
- Dedicator = Lucius Hispanius Fronto
- References = Tranoy 1981:304; CIRG II, no.115; CIL II 5612; IRG III, 16; Blázquez 1962: 115; ILER 684.

21. Mars Tarbucelis
- 'Coporici / Materni / ex voto / Marti Tar/buceli fu(l)/lones' (AE 1983:562).
- Location = Montariol, S. Vitor (Palmeira, Braga)
- Dedicators = The fullers of the region of Braga
- References = AE 1983:562; Tranoy 1981:304.

22. Nymphae Lupianae
- 'Antonia Rufina voto Ninphis Lupianis libens animo posuit' (Santos Junior & Cardozo 1953:61).
- Location = Tagilde (Guimarâes)
- Dedicator = Antonia Rufina
- References = Blázquez 1962:177; Tranoy 1981:304; Santos Junior & Cardozo 1953:61; CIL II 6288; Encarnação 1975:224-6; ILER 696.

23. Nymphae Silonae
- 'Nymphis / Silonis A(ula) / Cloviana ex voto f(aciendum) c(urauit)' (Rodríguez Colmenero 1977:303). This is interpreted as: 'Nimphis Silonsaclo/viana ex voto f.c.' in CIL II 5625. Tranoy prefers to separate the second word and get 'Cloutiana' or 'Cloutana' as the dedicator (Tranoy 1981:325). IRG IV, 77 has: 'Silon(i)s Acloviana.'
- Location = Alongos
- Dedicator = Cloutina/Cloviana
- References = Tranoy 1981:325; Rodríguez Colmenero 1977:303; CIL II 5625; IRG IV, 77.

24. Tutela Berisus
- ' Tutella[e] (sic) / Berisi / Silo Silo/nis / v(otum) s(oluit) l(ibens) m(erito)' (AE 1981, 537).
- Location = S. Vicente de Concieiro, Paderne, Orense.
- Dedicator = Silo Silonis?
- References = AE 1981, 537.

25. Tutela Tiriensis
- 'Tutelae Tiri/ensi Pompei (filius) / Clitus / Corinthu(s) / Calvinus / ex voto' (Blázquez 1962:63).
- Location = S. María de Ribeira (Pinhâo, Sabrosa).
- Dedicators = Three freedmen, with the respective cognomens Clitus, Corinthus and Calvinus, all of the gens Pompeius (Tranoy 1981:301), though Blázquez has Pompeus as the father's name (1962:63).
- References = Blázquez 1962:63; Tranoy 1981:305; ILER 703; Leite de Vasconcelos 1905:197-8; Encarnaçâo 1975:294-6.

Uncertain Readings from the Conventus Bracaraugustanus

26. Lares Varigis?
- '[Laribus] / Vari/gis V/lac(ius) So/usen(us) / v(otum) s(oluit) l(ibens) m(erito)' (AE 1987, 562f).
- Location = Rabal, Oimbra (Orense)
- Dedicator = Ulacius Sousenus
- References = AE 1987, 562f.

27. Nymphis Castaecis (?)
- 'Reburrinus Lapidarius (Nymphis) Castaecis v(otum) l(ibens) (soluit) m(erito)' (Santos Junior & Cardozo 1953:61).
- Location = Santa Eulália de Barrosas, Concelho de Lousada (Porto).
- Dedicator = Reburrinus Lapidarius
- References = Santos Junior & Cardozo 1953:61; CIL II 2404.

Conventus Lucensis

28. Genius Castelli
- 'Genio / Caste/lli Bl/oena / Sabin/i (filia) v(otum) l(ibens) s(oluit)' (CIRG I, no.67).
- Location = Found in 1984 in a church at Cores, Ponteceso.
- Dedicator = Bloena, daughter of Sabinus.
- References = CIRG I, no.67; AE 1992, 998.

* See Lares Callaeci in an inscription to Venus Victrix, etc (No.182, Cat.II)

Uncertain Reading from the Conventus Lucense

29. Domino (Cosus?)
- 'Domi/no [---] / [---] / [---]' (CIRG II, no.129 - In which Baños Rodríguez suggests it
- may have been to Dominus Cosus as Cosus is prone to taking Deus or Dominus and is frequently evidenced in the North-west).
- Location = Found buried in the church of Santa María de Curro, Barro
- Dedicator = Unknown
- References = CIRG II, no.129

Conventus Austurum

30. Genius of the Fons Sag... (or Fontis Agineesis).
- 'Fonti Sag[in<i>Geno] / Brocci L(ucius) Ulp(ius) S(exti) f(ilius) / Alexis Aguilegus/ v(otum) s(oluit) l(ibens) m(erito)' (HE 1989, no.385). Difficult to decipher, this deity name was early translated as 'Genius Broccus' (CIL II 2694). Quintana Prieto has 'Fontis Ag[inees(is) Genio]' (1969:60-2). Blázquez (1962:168) and ILER 656 have: 'Fontis Aginees(is) Genio.'
- Location = Boñar (León).
- Dedicator = Lucius Ulpius son of Sextus
- References = Tranoy 1981:305-6; HE 1989, no.385; CIL II 2694 and 5726; Blázquez 1962:168; Quintana Prieto 1969:60-2; ILER 656.

31. Jupiter Candamius
- 'Iovi Candamio' (Pastor Muñoz 1976:499).
- Location = The mountainous zone of the north of the province of León, in the region of the hills of Pajares and of Piedrafita. Likely from the community Candanedo de Fenar, near La Robla (Albertos Frimat 1974:152).
- Dedicator = Unknown
- References = Tranoy 1981:306; Pastor Muñoz 1976:499;CIL II 2695; Blázquez 1962:87; ILER 666; Albertos Firmat 1974:151-2.

32. Jupiter Ladicus
- 'Iovi La/dico M(arcus) / Ulp(ius) Aug(usti) lib(ertus) Gr/acilis / ex voto' (IRG IV, 63). Tranoy takes this as: 'Iov O M/Digo' or I.O.M. Digus (Tranoy 1981:306).
- Location = Codos de Larouco (Larouco), Orense.
- Dedicator = Marcus Ulpius Gracilis, freedman.
- References = AE 1977, 445; Pastor Muñoz 1976:500; IRG IV, 63; Tranoy 1981:306; CIL II 2525; Blázquez 1962:88; ILER 671.

33. Jupiter Ladicus
- 'Iovi (sic) [La]dico Iu/lius Gr/acilis / ex vot(o)' (AE 1977, 445).
- Location = Codos de Larouco (Larouco), Orense.
- Dedicator = Iulius Gracilis
- References = AE 1977, 445; IRG IV, 62.

34. Mars Tilenus
- 'Marti / Tileno' (Mañanez Perez 1982:no.121). Inscribed on a silver plaque.
- Location = Quintana del Marco (La Bañeza).
- Dedicator = Unknown
- References = Tranoy 1981:306; Mañanez Perez 1982:no.121; Blázquez 1962:126; Albertos Firmat 1974:150; Pastor Muñoz 1976:517; ILER 687; EE IX, 293.

35. Tutela Bolgensis
- 'Tutelae / Bongens(i) / Claudius / Capito / pro s(alute) s(ua) et / s(uorum) p(osuit) ex vo(to)' (Blázquez 1962:63).
- Location = Cacabelos (Ponferrada)
- Dedicator = Claudius Capito
- References = Blázquez 1962:63; Tranoy 1981:306; ILER 700.

36. Tutela Cal(purniorum)
- 'Flaccus / Avit(i) Tute/lae Cal(purniorum) vot(um) / l(ibens) sol(uit) pr(o) filio' (AE 1994, 962).
- Location = Rodanillo, Astorga, León.
- Dedicator = Falccus, son of Avitus?
- References = AE 1994, 962; Otherwise unpublished.

37. Serapis Sanctus, Isis Mirionima, Core Invicta, Apollo Grannus, Mars Sagatus
- 'Serapidi / Sancto / Isidi Mironymo / Core Invictae / Apollini Granno / Marti Sagato / Iul(ius) Melanio / proc(urator) Augg(ustorum) v. s. /' (Pastor Muñoz 1976:502).
- Location = Conventus of Astorga
- Dedicator = Julius Melanius, Imperial procurator
- References = Tranoy 1981:314; Mañanez Perez 1982:no.16; Pastor Muñoz 1976:502; Quintana Prieto 1969:42; AE 1968, 230.

Location Unsure in the North-West

38. Dii Ceceaigi
- 'Diis Cec/eaigi / Iriba / Mrcu / saftu/ri' (CIL II 2597).
- Location = Imprecise location in north-west Iberia.
- Dedicator = Interpreted as Marcus A[e]turi (CIL II 2597).
- References = Tranoy 1981:304; CIL II 2597; Blázquez 1962:131.

39. Jupiter Optimus Maximus Anderon
- 'I.O.M. / Anderon / M Ulpius / Aug lib / Eutyches proc/ metall alboc' (CIL II 2598).
- Location = Imprecise location in north-west Iberia.
- Dedicator = A freedmen under Trajan, M. Ulpius Eutychès in charge of a mining sector (procurator metallorum).
- References = Tranoy 1981:305; Blazquez 1962:97; CIL II 2598; ILER 664.

40. Jupiter Optimus Maximus Candiedus
- 'I(ovi) O(ptimo) M(aximo) / Candiedoni / T(itus) Caesius Rufus / Saelenus / ex voto fecit' (Pastor Muñoz 1976:499).
- Location = Imprecise location in north-west Iberia.
- Dedicator = T. Caesius Rufus (of Asturian origin, and of the people called the Saelini) (Tranoy 1981:305).
- References = Tranoy 1981:305; Pastor Muñoz 1976:499; CIL II 2599; Blázquez 1962: 87; Albertos Firmat 1974:149-50; ILER 667.

• Dedications for which the reading of the inscription is either unpublished or could not be located by the researcher.

Appendix I

1. Indigenous Insriptions from Catalogue I

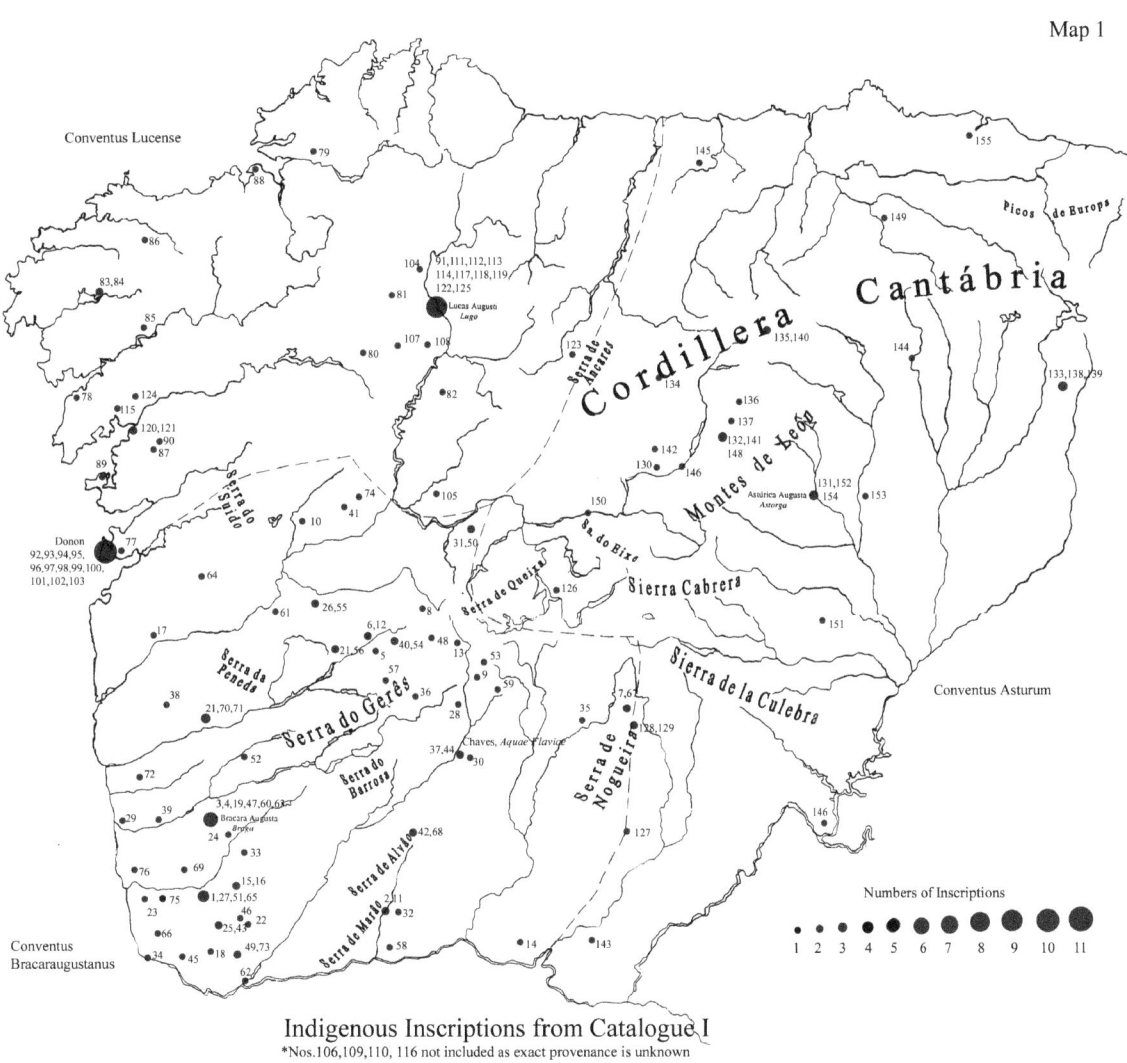

Indigenous Inscriptions from Catalogue I
*Nos.106,109,110, 116 not included as exact provenance is unknown

2. Roman Inscriptions from Catalogue II

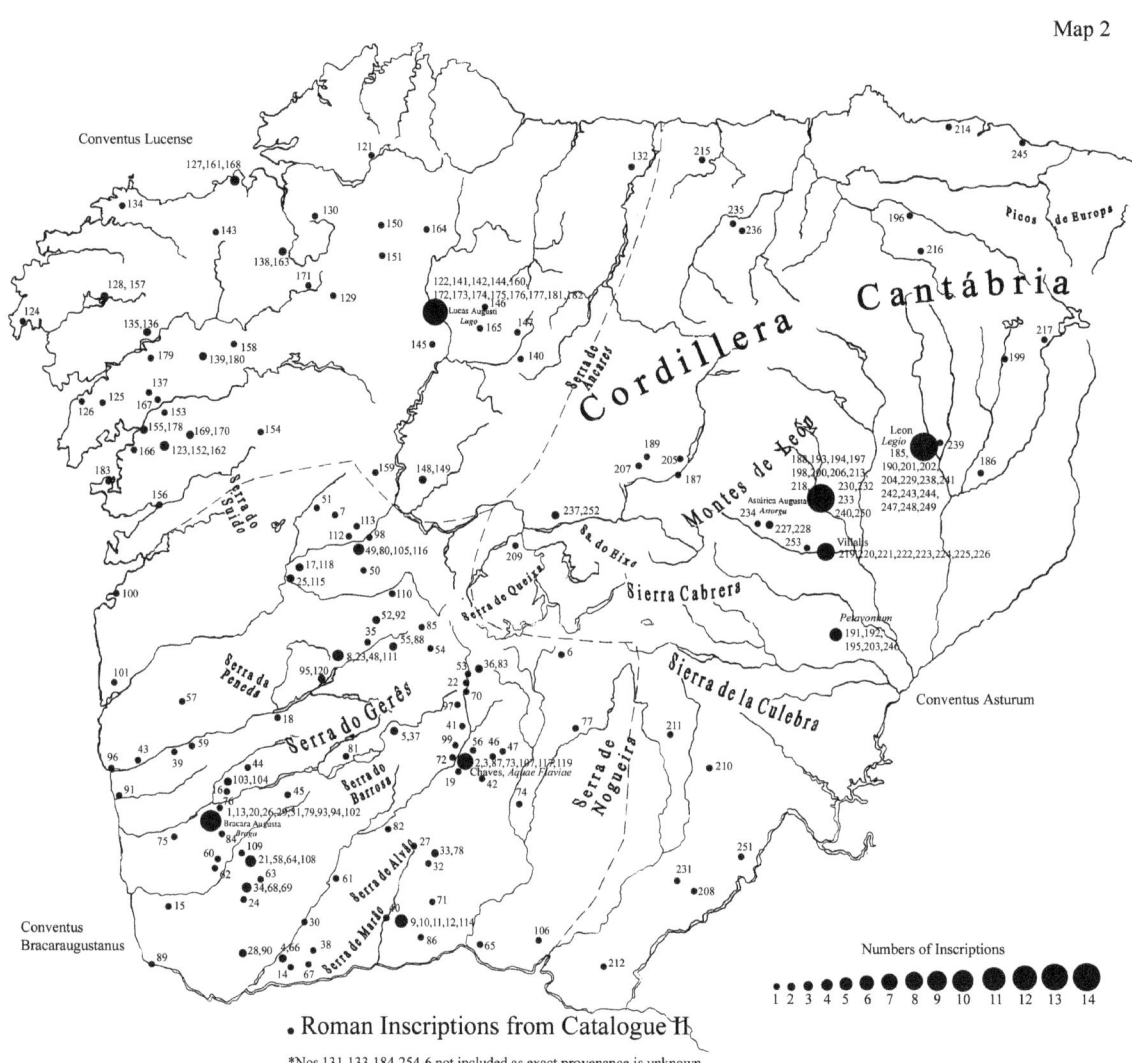

Map 2

3. Roman Inscriptions with Indigenous Epithets from Catalogue III

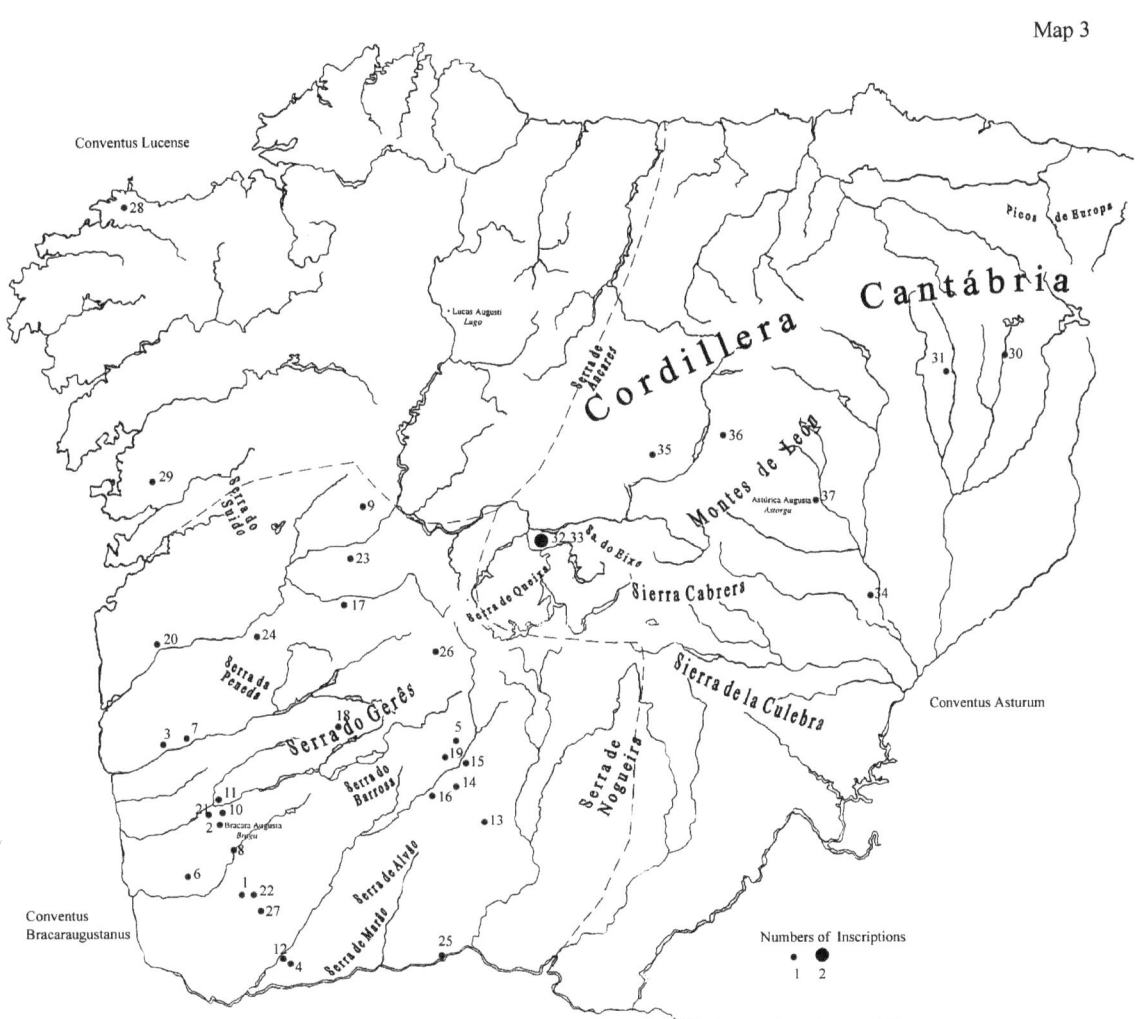

• Roman Inscriptions with Indigenous Epithets from Catalogue III
* Nos. 38-40 not included as exact provenance is unknown

4. Reve Inscriptions from Catalogue I

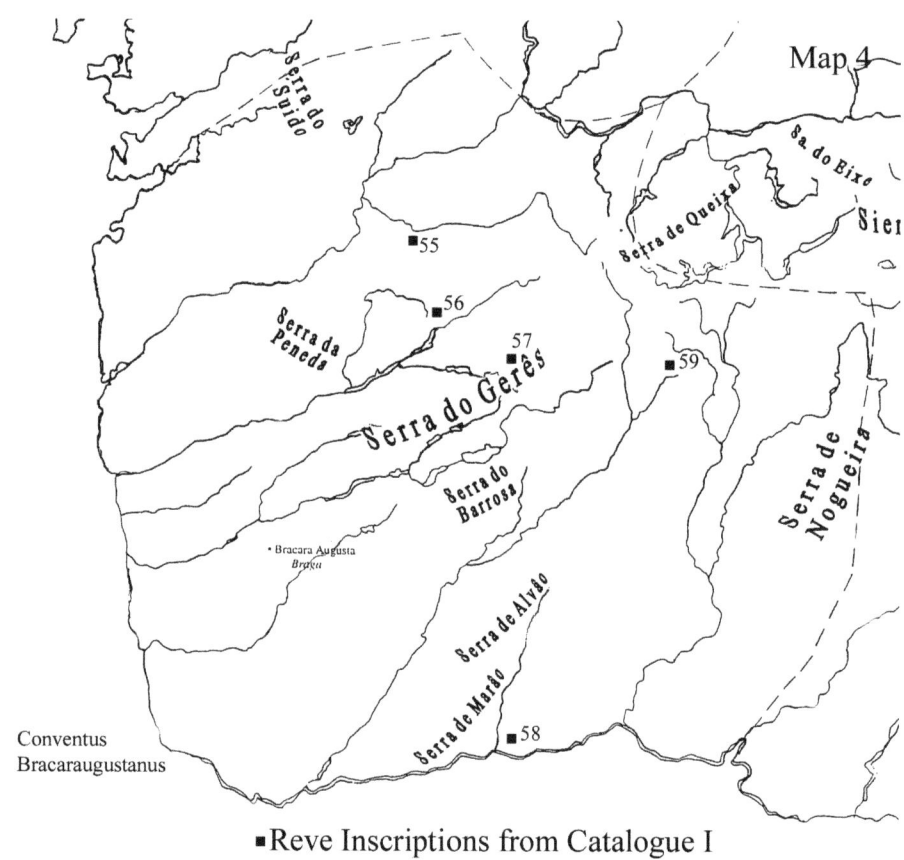

■Reve Inscriptions from Catalogue I

5. Jupiter Inscriptions from Catalogues I, II, and III

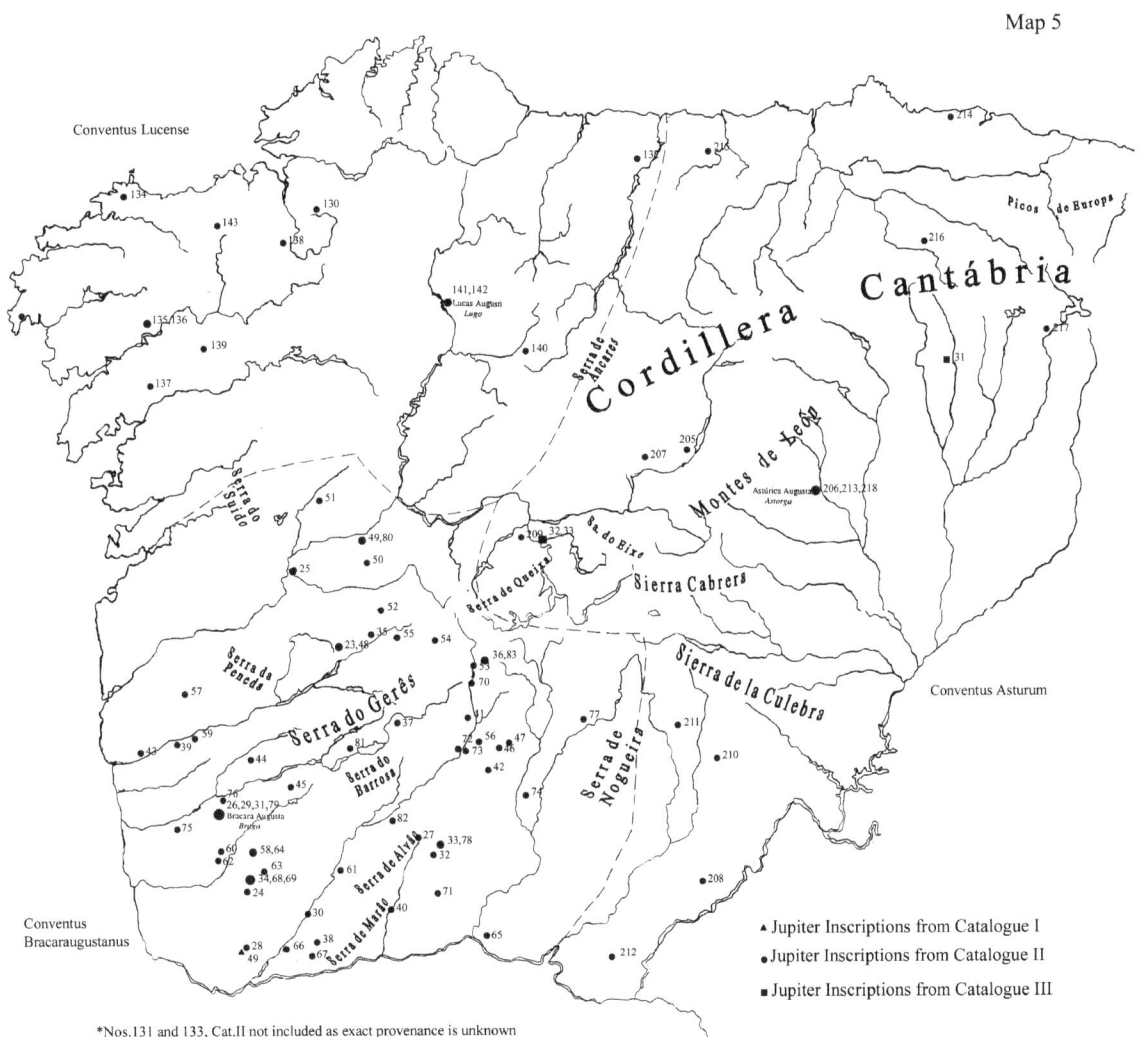

Map 5

*Nos.131 and 133, Cat.II not included as exact provenance is unknown
*Dedications which also venerate the Emperor or have Latin epithets such as Capitolinus are not included (Nos.84-7,144,219-234,Cat.II).

ELEMENTS OF NATIVE RELIGION IN THE NORTH-WEST OF THE IBERIAN PENINSULA

6. Nabia Inscriptions from Catalogue I

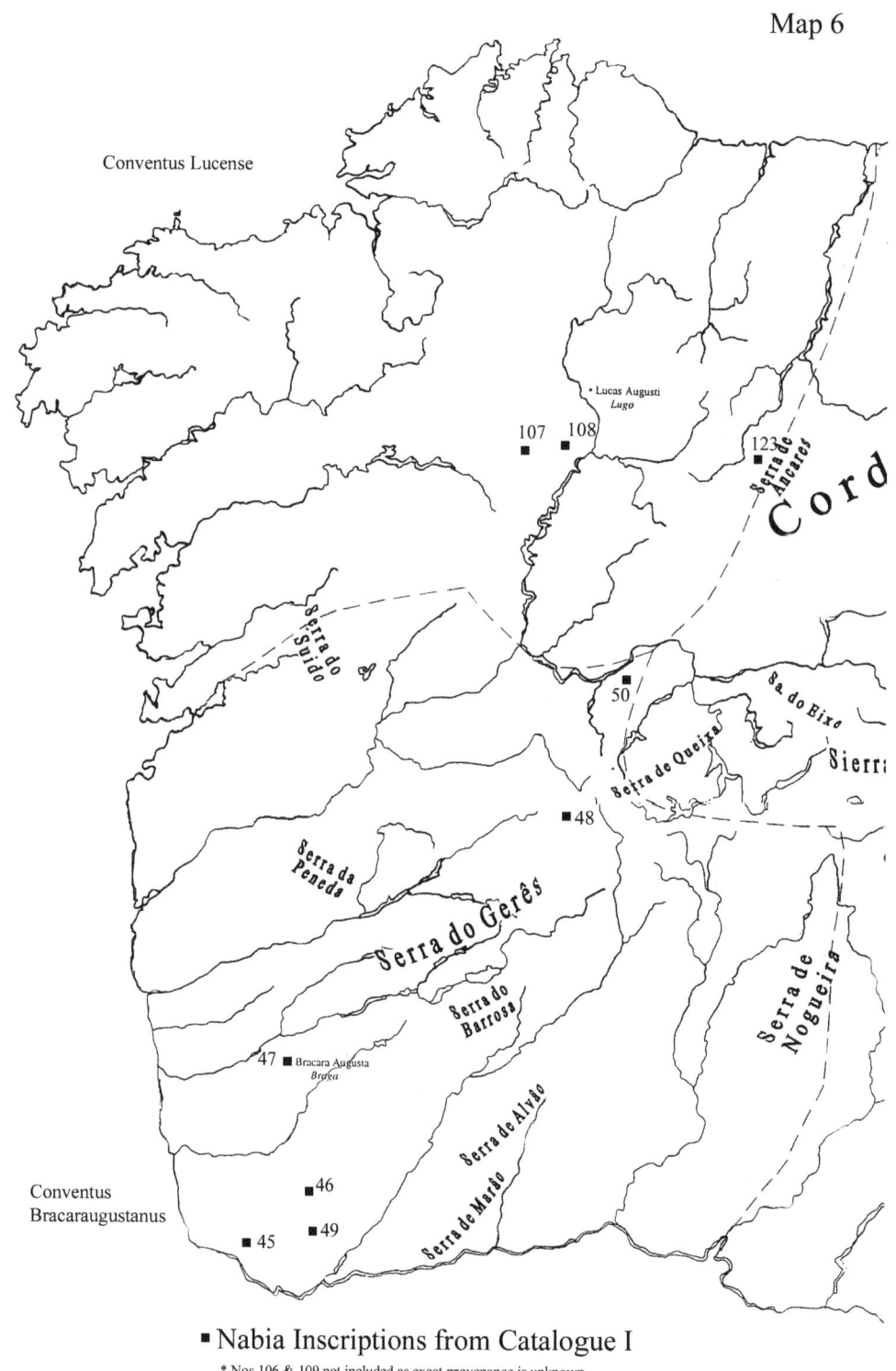

Map 6

■ Nabia Inscriptions from Catalogue I
* Nos.106 & 109 not included as exact provenance is unknown

7. Nymph Inscriptions from Catalogue II and III

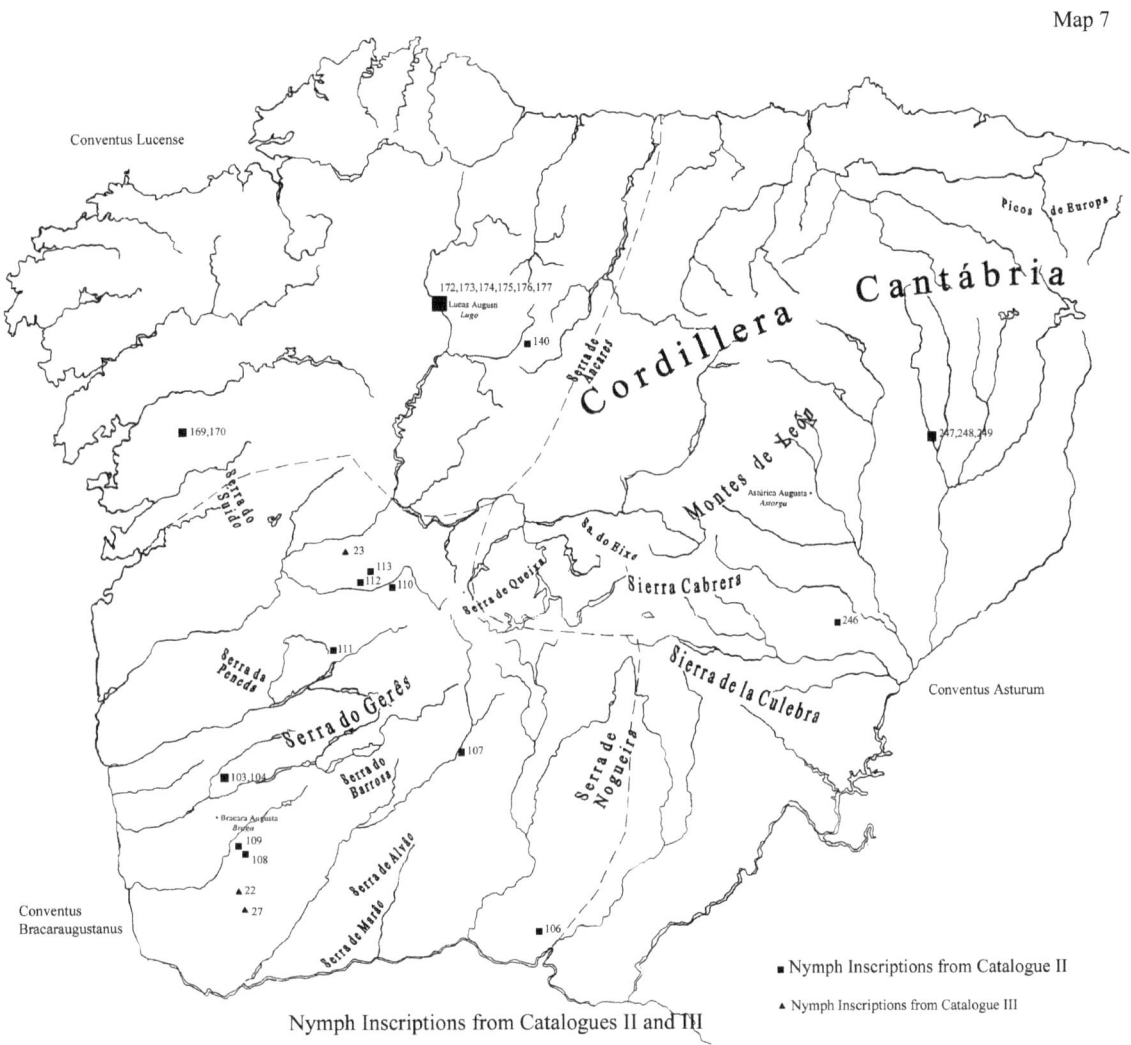

Map 7

Nymph Inscriptions from Catalogues II and III

■ Nymph Inscriptions from Catalogue II
▲ Nymph Inscriptions from Catalogue III

8. Bandua Inscriptions from Catalogue I

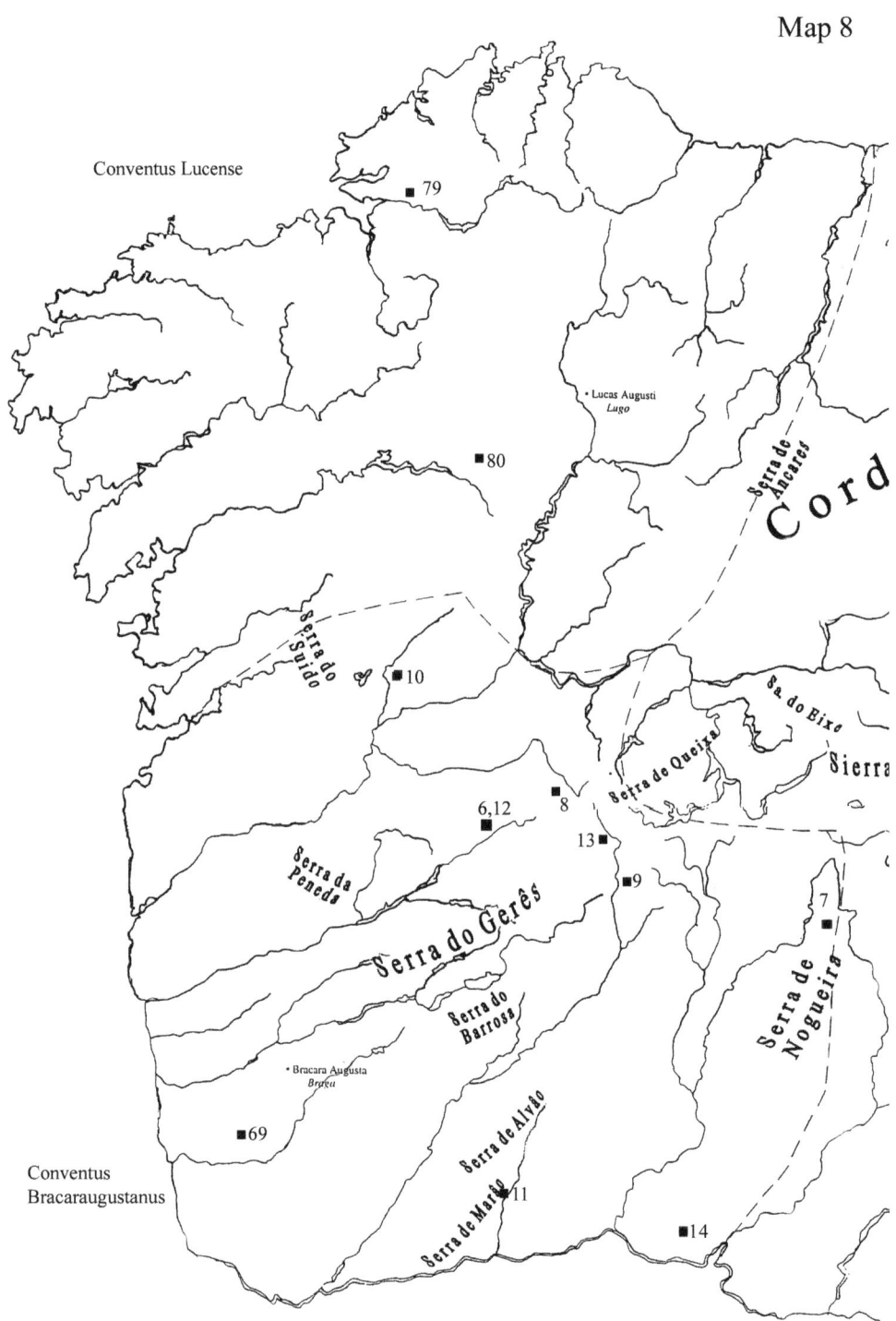

Map 8

■ Bandua Inscriptions from Catalogue I

9. Lar, Lares and Lares Viales Inscriptions from Catalogues II and III

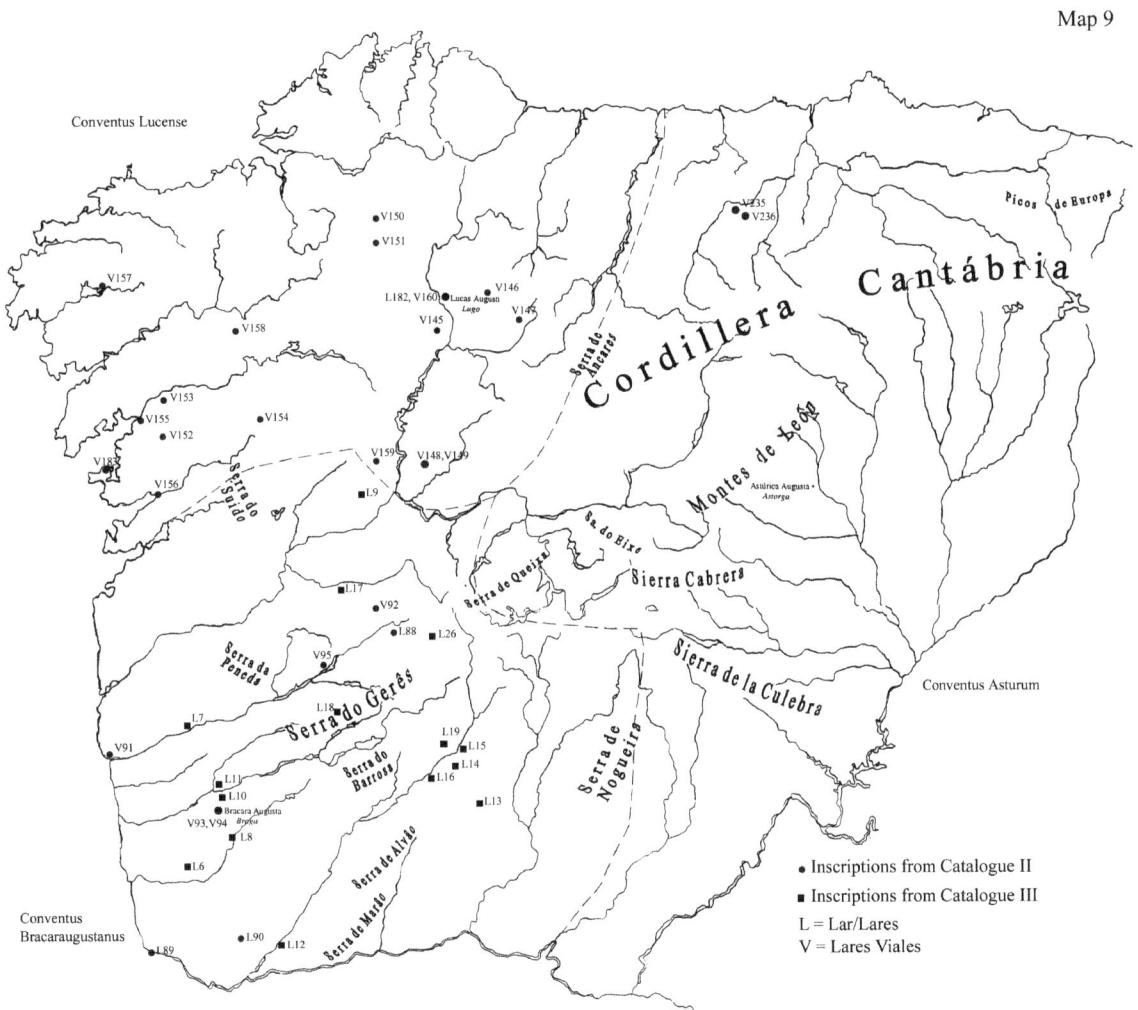

Lar, Lares and Lares Viales Inscriptions from Catalogues II & III
*No.184, Cat.II not included as exact provenance is unknown

10. Cosus Inscriptions from Catalogue I

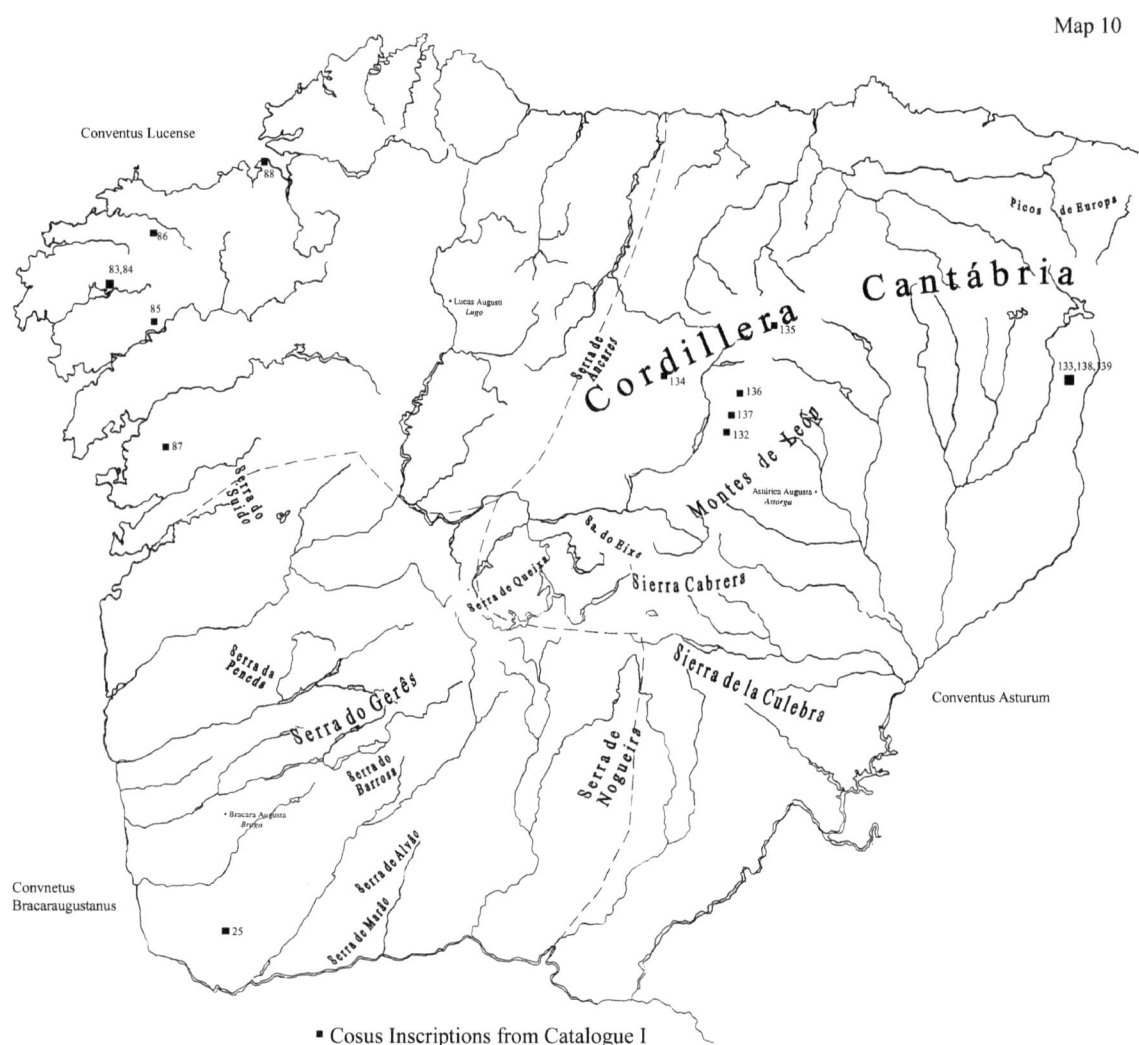

Map 10

■ Cosus Inscriptions from Catalogue I

11. Mars Inscriptions from Catalogues II and III

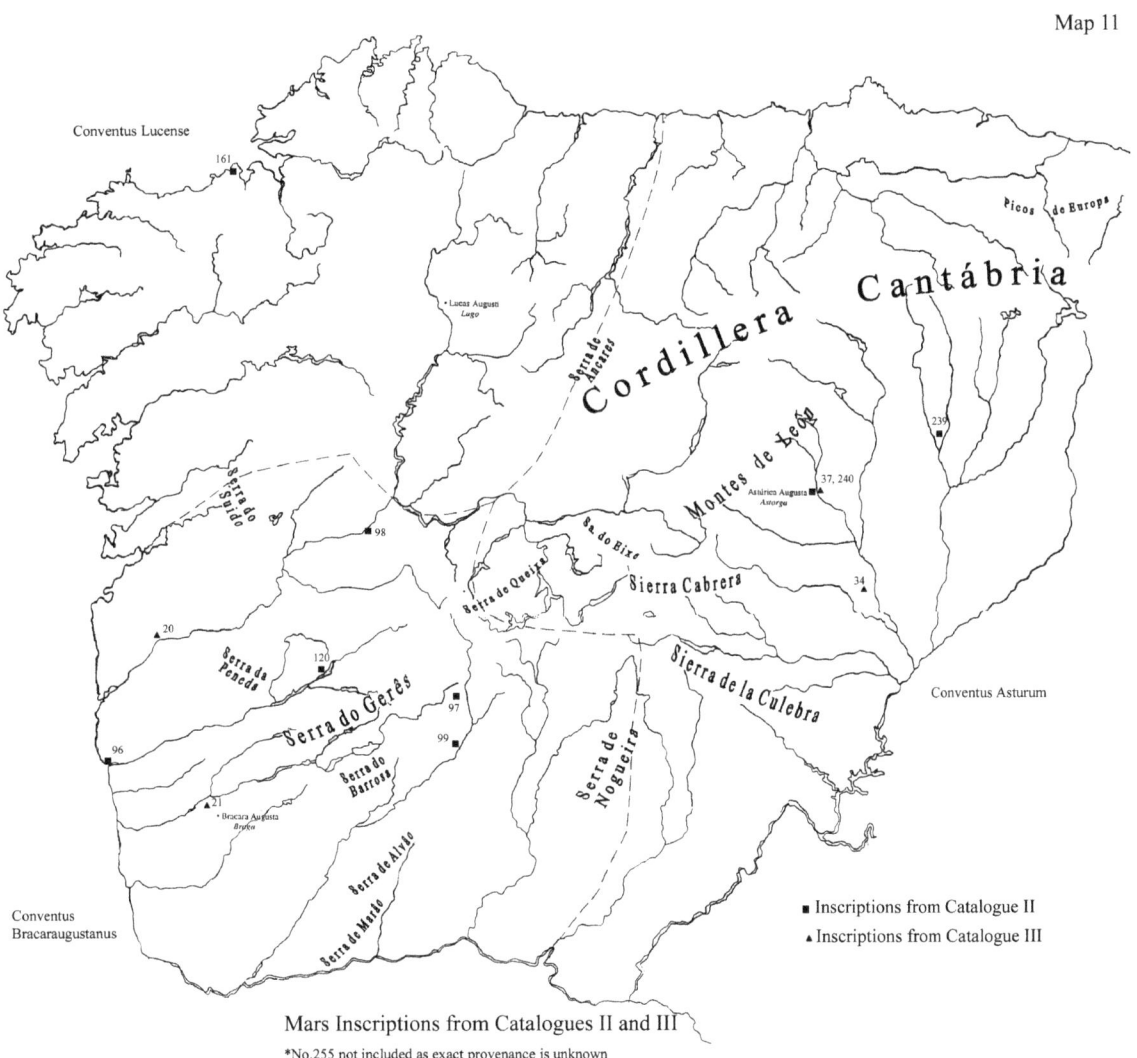

Mars Inscriptions from Catalogues II and III
*No.255 not included as exact provenance is unknown

References

Alarcâo, J. de (1988), *Roman Portugal*, Vols. I-III, English Edition, Warminster.

Albertos Firmat (1974), 'El Culto a los Montes entre los Galaicos, Astures y Berones y Algunas Deidades Más Signicativas,' *Estudios de Arqueoogía Alavesa*, Vol.6, pp.147-157.

Alcock, J.P. (1965), 'Celtic Water Cults in Roman Britain,' *Archaeological Journal*, Vol.122, pp.1-12.

Allason-Jones, L. & B. McKay (1985), *Coventina's Well: A Shrine on Hadrian's Wall*, Oxford.

Alvorado Gonzalo, M. et al. (1998), 'El templo romano de Collado de Piedras Labradas (Jarilla, Cáceres), in *Homenaje a José Mª Blázquez, Vol.V, Hispania Romana II*, Ed. J. Alvar, Madrid, pp.1-19.

Arias Vilas, F., P. Le Roux, & A. Tranoy (1979), *Inscriptions romaines de la province de Lugo*, Paris.

Balil, A. (1979), 'Esculturas de Época Romana en Galicia (Aspectos y Problemas),' *Revista de Guimarâes*, Vol.88, pp.1-13.

Baños, G. & G. Pereira-Menaut (1998), 'Deus Larius Breus Brus Sanctus. Las Inscripciones Votivas del Facho de Donón (Pontevedra),' in *Homenaje a José Mª Blázquez, Vol. V, Hispania Romana II*, Ed. Jaime Alvar, Madrid, pp.21-44.

Beltrán Lloris, F. (1992), 'Culto a los Lares y Grupos de Parentesco en le Hispania Indoeuropea,' in *Religio Deorum: Actas del Coloquio Internacional de Epigrafía Culto y Soceidad en Occidente*, Ed. M. Mayer, Barcelona, pp.59-71.

Bermejo Barrera, J.C. (1978), *La Sociedad en la Galicia Castreña*, Santiago.

Birley, E. (1986), 'The Deities of Roman Britain,' *Aufstieg und Niedergang der Römischen Welt*, II, 18.1, Berlin, pp.3-112.

Blanco Freijeiro, A. 1977, *El Puente de Alcantara en su Contexto Historico*, Madrid.

Blázquez, J.M. (1962), *Religiones Primitivas de Hispania. I. Fuentes literarias y Epigráficas*, Madrid.

(1970), 'Las religiones indígenas del area noroeste de la Penínsule Ibérica en relación con Roma,' in *Legio VII Gemina*, León, pp.63-77.

(1975), *Diccionario de las religiones prerromanas de Hispana*, Madrid.

(1983), *Primitivas Religiones Ibericas: Tomo II, Religiones Prerromanas*, Madrid.

(1991), *Religiones en la España Antigua*, Madrid.

(2001), Religiones, ritos y creencias funerarias de la Hispania Prerromana, Madrid.

Bouza-Brey, F. (1946), 'Vestio Alonieco, Nueva Deidad Galaica,' *Archivo Español de Arqueología*, Vol.19, pp.110-116.

Caridad Arias, J. (1999), *Cultos y Divinidades de la Galicia Prerromana, a través de la Toponimia*, La Coruña.

Curchin, L.A. (1991), *Roman Spain: Conquest and Assimilation*, London.

(2004), *The Romanization of Central Spain: Complexity, Diversity and Change in a Provincial Hinterland*, London.

Diez de Velasco, F. de P. (1985), 'Balnearios y Dioses de las Aguas Termales en Galicia Romana,' *Archivo Español de Archaeologia*, Vol.58, pp.69-98.

Encarnaçâo, J, d' (1975), *Divinidades Indígenas sob o dominio romano em Portugal*, Lisbon.

Fabre, G. (1992), 'Les Divinites "Indigenes" en Aquitaine Meridionale sous l'Empire Romain,' in *Religio deorum: Actas del Coloquio Internacional de Epigrafía Culto y Sociedad en Occidente*, Ed. M. Mayer, Barcelona, pp.177-191.

Fernández Castro, M.C. (1995), *Iberia in Prehistory*, Oxford.

Fouet, G & A. Souton (1963), 'Une cime pyrénéenne consacreé à Jupiter: Le Mont-Sacon (Htes-Pyrénées),' *Gallia*, Vol.21, pp.275-294.

García y Bellido, A (1966), 'Nuevos documentos militares de la Hispania romana,' *Archivo Español de Arqueologia*, Vol.39, pp.24-40.

(1971), 'Parerga de arqueología y epigrafía hispano-romana IV, *Archivo Español de Arqueología*, Vol.44, pp.137-151.

Green, M. (1986), *The Gods of the Celts*, Gloucester.

González Pardo, I.M. (1965), 'Conjeturas etimologicas sobre teonimos Galaicos,' *Archivo Español de Arqueología*, Vol.38, pp.50-4.

Hassall, M.W.C. & R.S.O. Tomlin (1978), 'Roman Britain in 1977: II. Inscriptions,' *Britannia*, Vol.9, pp.473-504.

Herves Raigoso, F. & G. Meijide Cameselle (2000), 'Les Nymphes des Thermes,' *Gallaecia*, Vol.19, pp.187-196.

James, S. (2001), '"Romanization" and the peoples of Britain,' in *Italy and the West: Comparative Issues in*

Romanization, Eds. S. Keay & N. Terrenato, Oxford, pp.187-209.

Jufer, N. & T. Luginbühl (2001), *Répertoire des Dieux Gaulois: les noms des divinités Celtiques connus par l'epigraphie, les texts antiques et la toponymie*, Paris.

Keay, S.J. (1988), *Roman Spain*, London.

—— (2001), 'Romanization and the Hispaniae,' in *Italy and the West: Comparative Issues in Romanization*, Eds. S. Keay & N. Terrenato, Oxford, pp.117-144.

Lambrino, S. (1965), 'Les Cultes Indigènes en Espagne sous Trajan et Hadrien,' in *Les Empereurs Romains d'Espagne*, Eds. M.A. Piganiol & H. Terasse, Paris, pp.223-242.

Leite de Vasconcelos, J (1905), *Religiôes da Lusitana*, II, Lisbon.

—— (1913), *Religôes da Lusitana*, III, Lisbon.

Lenerz-de Wilde, M. (1995), 'The Celts in Spain,' in *The Celtic World*, Ed. M.J. Green, London.

Le Roux, P & A. Tranoy (1973), 'Rome et les indigenes dans le nord-ouest de la Peninsule Iberique. Problemes d'epigraphie et d'histoire,' in *Melanges de la Casa de Velazquez*, Paris, Vol.9, pp.177-231.

López Cuevillas, F (1988), *La Civilizacion Celtica en Galicia*, New Edition (Original 1953), Madrid.

Lourenço Fontes, A (1980), 'Culto ao Deus Larouco, Jupiter e Ategina,' in *Actas do Seminário de Arqueologia do Noroeste Peninsular*, Vol. III, Revista de Guimarâes, Guimarâes, pp.5-20.

Lourenço Fontes, A & A. Rodríguez Colmenero (1980), 'El Culto a los Montes entre los Galaico-Romanos,' in *Actas do Seminário de Arqueologia do Noroeste Peninsular*, Vol. III, Revista de Guimarâes, Guimarâes, pp.21-36.

Mangas, J. (1995), 'Religión del Area Astur,' in *Astures: Pueblos y Culturas en la Frontera del Imperio Romano*, C. Fernández Ochoa et al, Gijón, pp.159-169.

—— (1998), 'Pervivencias Sociales de Astures y Cántabros en los Modelos Administrativos Romanos: Tiempo y Modos,' in *Romanización y Reconquista en la Península Ibérica: Nuevas Perspectivas*, Eds. Mª J. Hidalgo, D. Pérez & M. J. R. Gervás, Salamanca, pp.117-128.

Mangas, J & M. Olano (1995), 'Nueva inscripción latina, castella y castellani del área Astur,' *Gerión*, Vol.13, pp.339-347.

Mañanez Perez, T. (1982), 'Epigrafia Y Numismatica de Astorga Romana y su Entorno,' in *Acta Salmanticensia*, Vol.134, pp.1-292 (all pages).

Marco Simón, F. (1992), 'La individuación del espacio sagrado: Testimonios cultuales en el noroeste Hispanico,' in *Religio Deorum: Actas del Coloquio Internacional de Epigrafía Culto y Soceidad en Occidente*, Ed. M. Mayer, Barcelona, pp.317-324.

Mayer, M. & I. Rodà (1986), 'Les divinités feminines de la fertilité et de la fécondité en Hispania pendant l'époque romaine' in *Archaeology and Fertility Cult in the Ancient Mediterranean*, Ed. A. Bonanno, Malta, pp.293-304.

Millett, M. (1990), 'Romanization: Historical Issues and Archaeological Interpretation,' in *The Early Roman Empire in the West*, Eds. T. Blagg & M. Millett, Oxford, Chpt.4, pp.35-44.

Nicols, J. (1987), 'Indigenous Culture and the Process of Romanization in Iberian Galicia,' *The American Journal of Philology*, Vol.108, no.1, pp.127-151.

Olivares Pedreño, J.C. (2000a), 'Los dioses sobernos y los ríos en la religion indígena de la Hispania indoeuropea,' *Gerión*, Vol.18, pp.191-212.

—— (2000b) 'Los dioses indígenas en el Noroeste de Portugal,' *Conimbriga*, Vol.39, pp.53-83.

Parente, J. (1980), 'Subsidios inéditos, para a historia de Trêsminas' in *Actas do Seminário de Arqueologia do Noroeste Peninsular*, Vol. III, Guimarâes, pp.131-40.

Pastor Muñoz, M. (1976), 'La Religión Romana en el Conventus Asturum,' *Hispania*, Vol. 36, no.134, pp.489-524.

Prieur, J. (1976), 'L'histoire des regions alpestres (Alpes Maritimes, Cottiennes, Graies et Pennines) sous le haut-empire romain (Ier –IIIe siècle après J.C.),' in *Aufstieg und Niedergang der Römischen Welt*, II, 5.2, Berlin, pp.630-656.

Quintana Prieto, A. (1969), 'La Religion Pagana en Tierras de León,' in *Archivos Leonenses*, Vol.23, pp.33-107.

Ramirez, J.L. (1981), 'Las Creencias Religiosas, Pervivencia Ultima de las Civilizaciones Prerromanas en la Peninsula Iberica,' in *La Religion Romana en Hispania*, Madrid, pp.223-252.

Rico, C. (1997), *Pyrénées Romaines: Essai sur un pays de frontière (IIIe siècle av. J.C. – IVe siècle ap. J.C.)*, Madrid.

Rodríguez Colmenero, A. (1977), *Galicia Meridional Romana*, Bilbao (Madrid).

—— (1993), *Corpus-Catalogo de Inscripciones Rupestres de Epoca Romana del Cuadrante Noroccidental de la Peninsula Iberica*, La Coruña.

Rodríguez Colmenero, A & A. Lourenço Fontes (1980), 'El culto a los montes entre los Galaico-Romanos, in *Actas do Seminário de Arqueologia do Noroeste Peninsular*, Vol.III, Guimarâes, pp.21-36.

Ross, A. (1992), *Pagan Celtic Britain: Studies in Iconography and Tradition*, Revised Edition, London.

Santos Junior, J.R. dos, & M. Cardozo (1953), 'Ex-Votos às Ninfas em Portugal,' *Zephyrus*, Vol.4, pp.53-68.

Santos Yanguas, N. (1991), *La Romanizacion de Asturias*, Madrid.

Savory, H.N. (1968), *Spain and Portugal: The Prehistory of the Iberian Peninsula*, London.

Sopeña Genzor, Gabriel (1995), *Etnica y Ritual: Aproximación al estudio de la Religiosidad de los Pueblos Celtiberos*, Zaragoza.

Thevenot, E (1968), *Divinités et Sanctuaires de la Gaule*, Paris.

Tovar, A. (1964-5), 'L'inscription du Cabeço das Fráguas et la langue de Lusitaniens,' *Études Celtiques*, XI, pp.238-268.

(1989), 'Las Tribus y las Ciudades de la Antigua Hispania, Segunda Parte, Tomo 3: Tarraconensis,' in *Iberische Landeskunde*, Strasbourgh.

Tovar, A. & Blázquez, J.M. (1975), *Historia de la Hispania Romana: La Península Ibérica desde 218 a.c. hasta el siglo V*, Tercera Parte, Madrid.

Tranoy A. (1980), 'Religion et Société à Bracara Augusta (Braga) au Haut-Empire Romain,' in *Actas do Seminário de Arqueologia do Noroeste Peninsular*, Vol. III, Revista de Guimarâes, Guimarâes, pp.67-83.

(1981), *La Galice Romaine: Recherches sur le nord-ouest de la peninsula Ibérique dans l'Antiquité*, Paris.

Untermann, J. (1965), 'Miscelaneas epigrafico-lingüísticas: Inscripción de la Pedra Escrita del Castro de Tres Ríos (Viseu)' *Archivo Español de Arqueología*, Vol.38, pp.8-18.

Van Andringa, W. (2002), *La Religion en Gaule Romaine: Piété et Politique (Ier – IIIe Siècle apr. J.C.)*, Paris.

Vázquez Varela, J.M. & F. Acuña Castroviejo (1992), 'Pervivencia de las Formas Culturales Indigenas,' in *La Romanización de Galicia*, F. Acuña Castroviejo et al, La Coruña.

Vilas, A., P. Le Roux & A. Tranoy (1979), *Inscriptions Romaines de la Province de Lugo*, Paris.

Villar, F. (1994-5), 'Marandigui. Un Nuevo Epíteto de la Divinidad Lusitana Reve,' *Beiträge zur Namenforschung*, Vol.29-30, pp.247-255.

Vigil, M (1961), 'Ala II Flavia Hispanorum Civium Romanorum,' *Archivo Español de Arqueología*, Vol.34, pp.104-8.

Webster, J. (1995), 'Interpretatio: Roman Word power and the Celtic Gods,' *Britannia*, Vol.26, pp.153-161.

Webster, G. (1986), *The British Celts and their Gods under Rome*, London.

Wheeler, R.E.M. & T.V. Wheeler (1932), 'Report on the Excavation of the Prehistoric, Roman and Post-Roman Site in Lydney Park, Gloucestershire,' *Reports of the Research Committee of the Society of Antiquaries of London*, No.IX, Oxford.

Wightman, E.M. 1970, *Roman Trier and the Treveri*, London.

Ancient Sources Quoted

Foster, B.O. (Trans.) (1929), *Livy: From the Founding of the City*, Vol. V, Books XXI-XXII.

Ker, W.C.A. (Trans.) (1930), *The Epigrams of Martial*, Vol.I, London.

Jones, H.L. (Trans.) (1923), *The Geography of Strabo*, Vol.II, London.

Abbreviated Sources

AE = *L'Année Epigraphique*

CIL = *Corpus Inscriptionum Latinarum*

CIRG I = Pereira Menaut, G. (1991), *Corpus de Inscripcions Romanas de Galicia, Vol.I, Provincia de A Coruña*, Santiago.

CIRG II = Baños Rodríguez, G. (1994), *Corpus de Inscripcions Romanas de Galicia, Vol.II, Provincia de Pontevedra*, Santiago.

EE VIII & IX= Hübner, E. (1899), 'Addimenta nova ad corporis Vol.II, in *Ephemeris Epigraphica*.

EE IX = Hübner, E. (1903), 'Addimenta nova ad corporis Vol.II, in *Ephemeris Epigraphica*.

ERA = Diego Santos, F. (1959), *Epigrafía romana de Asturias*, Oviedo.

HE = Mangas, J. et al. (1989), *Hispania Epigraphica*, I, Madrid.

ILER = Vives, J. (1971/2), *Inscripciones Latinas de la España Romana*, Barcelona.

IRG I = Bouza Brey, F. & A d'Ors (1949), *Inscripciones romanas de Galicia, I, Santiago de Compostela*, Santiago.

IRG II = Vázquez Saco, F & M. Vázquez Seijas, (1954), *Inscripciones romanas de Galicia, II, Provincia de Lugo*, Santiago.

IRG III = Figueira Valverde, J & A. d'Ors (1955),

Inscripciones romanas de Galicia, III, Museo de Pontevedra, Santiago.

IRG IV = Lorenzo Fernandez, J (Ed.) (1968), *Inscripciones romanas de Galicia, IV, Provincia de Orense*, Santiago.

RIB = Collingwood, R.G. & R.P.Wright (1995), *The Roman Inscriptions of Britain, I Inscriptions on Stone*, New Edition, Stroud, Gloucestershire.

*Sources in this bibliography refer to both the text and the three catalogues.

www.ingramcontent.com/pod-product-compliance
Ingram Content Group UK Ltd.
Pitfield, Milton Keynes, MK11 3LW, UK
UKHW061213180426
11947UKWH00029B/2035